The Workshop of the World

British Economic History from 1820 to 1880

OPUS 32 *Oxford Paperbacks University Series*

J. D. CHAMBERS

The Workshop of the World

British Economic History from 1820 to 1880

Second Edition

London
OXFORD UNIVERSITY PRESS
New York   Toronto

Oxford University Press

OXFORD   LONDON   NEW YORK

GLASGOW   TORONTO   MELBOURNE   WELLINGTON

CAPE TOWN   SALISBURY   IBADAN   NAIROBI   DAR ES SALAAM   LUSAKA   ADDIS ABABA

BOMBAY   CALCUTTA   MADRAS   KARACHI   LAHORE   DACCA

KUALA LUMPUR   SINGAPORE   HONG KONG   TOKYO

First published in the Home University Library *1961*
Second edition published as an Oxford University Press paperback 1968
Reprinted 1971

PRINTED IN GREAT BRITAIN AT THE UNIVERSITY PRESS, OXFORD
BY VIVIAN RIDLER, PRINTER TO THE UNIVERSITY

To my Wife

———————————————

Contents

Acknowledgements   ix

1 Introduction   1
   (i) Factors in the Transition to Machine
   Industry   1
   (ii) Industrial Society and the Coming
   of Machine Industry   12

2 The Advance of Machine Industry and
   Transport   18
   (i) Engineering, Textiles, Heavy
   Industry   18
   (ii) Railways, Shipping, Scientific
   Technology   35

3 Agriculture and the Corn Laws   46

4 Foreign Trade and Fiscal Policy   60

5 Banking, Credit, and Joint-Stock
   Enterprise   83

6 Years of Crisis   101

7 Population and the Growth of Towns   115

8   Labour in the 'Industry State'   130

Bibliography   154

Index   161

Acknowledgements

IN THE COURSE OF REVISION, I have contracted two additional obligations which call for grateful acknowledgements: to W. A. Armstrong for helpful suggestions regarding my treatment of population change and to Maurice Caplan for placing his local researches on post-1834 poor law administration so unreservedly at my disposal. Other small changes have been made in the light of new writing that has added to knowledge or deepened understanding of the period. The sources for these are indicated either in the form of footnotes in the text or in additions to the bibliography. I am also grateful to those, and especially to W. H. Chaloner, who pointed out the bibliographical errors of the first edition.

J. D. CHAMBERS

Nottingham, September 1967

1
Introduction

(i) *Factors in the Transition to Machine Industry*

THE PERIOD during which Britain can be described as the workshop of the world is open to a variety of definitions. In this book it is taken to lie roughly between the financial crisis of 1825 and the onset of what is known as the Great Depression in 1873, or in round figures, between 1820 and 1880. That is not to imply that by the last quarter of the century British economic supremacy was at an end; on the contrary, in some important respects it grew to a new peak of grandeur. It rested on the world-wide services Britain provided through her shipping and credit agencies and the mutually advantageous relations she had established with her dependent empire. By these means she was able to meet the gap between her exports and the imports which poured into her free market and thus to provide funds for the lubrication of the wheels of the world's commerce; but she no longer held a virtual monopoly of the supply of manufactured goods, and two vital components of her export trade consisted of raw materials: the products of her coal mines and the re-exported products of Australian ranches. Britain as the pioneer of the world industrial revolution had given place to Britain the world's banker, trader, and collier, and a competitor with other industrial giants whom she herself had materially assisted to adult stature.

At the beginning of the period so defined, Britain was in the throes of the transition (of which the earlier phases have been described in a previous volume[1] in this series) from a primarily agricultural

[1] T. S. Ashton, *The Industrial Revolution* (1948).

and commercial economy to a modern industrial state. For the first time in history, the life of a great nation had become geared to machine production for the international market; economic output over the long period was rising substantially faster than population growth and the foundation was being laid for a spectacular rise in the standard of living. It was the first transition of its kind, and since it was the product of natural growth and only marginally dependent on outside sources of capital and skill, it was also the last. Historians have sometimes complained that the change was managed badly; in view of the anxious efforts of undeveloped economies today to achieve the same end, the question to which historians are now more inclined to turn their attention is how it was managed at all.

In 1820, when this book takes up the story, the political face of the country remained unchanged though it reflected an entirely new mood; its geographical face, especially in the Midlands and North, appeared, to contemporaries, to be in process of transformation. In 1822, one of the earliest of the geological surveys reported that a traveller from London to the west or north-west would cross bands of clay and chalk and oolite and a broad zone of red marly sand, and beyond this he would find himself in the midst of coal mines and iron furnaces '—in South Wales, the Forest of Dean, the Black Country, in North Warwickshire and West Leicestershire and so through Nottinghamshire and Derbyshire to the coal and iron of Yorkshire and the North'. The Trent and Soar marked the eastern boundary, the Warwickshire Avon and the Severn the southern boundary, of the land of coal mines and iron furnaces. To the south of it most of the old industries were dying and, except in London, new ones were little more than desperate stop-gaps to take the place of the spinning and weaving and the metallurgical industries which in former times had been the staple of the industrial economy of the nation but which could no longer provide a return on capital or yield a livelihood to labour. To the north and west of it, a succession of startling successes had been won in the production of high quality goods at prices which brought them within the reach of constantly widening sectors of the market. Innovation had led to innovation, making possible an incalculable saving of time and labour and releasing circulating capital for investment in more machines or the production of more goods, 'a process', says Professor Ashton, 'which is at the centre of what is called the industrial revolution'.[1] Moreover, a major contribution to this vital process of transforming circulating into fixed capital had been made by the completion of a road system and a network of waterways which permitted the carriage of goods to all parts of the country with speed and safety and an absence of internal tolls that was known in no other country in Europe.

To a German visitor in 1828, Britain appeared to be an extraordinary land in which 'the new creations springing into life every year bordered on the fabulous'; a Frenchman walking through the Black Country on a dark night found the horizon 'bounded by a circle of fire. From all parts, columns of smoke and flame rose on the air and the whole country around seemed as if lighted by an intense conflagration.' An American visitor, after a tour of the northern textile towns and villages, spoke of the new workmen's stone cottages fresh from the mason's yards which met his eyes on every side.

These travellers could have found equally significant evidence of Britain's economic power nearer home. In 1789, an ambitious young man, Samuel Slater, quietly left his home in Belper and was next heard of in Pawtucket, Rhode Island, where he built a replica of the Arkwright machine from memory (since to take out plans was illegal) and so became the founder of the American power textile industry. The Cockerill Brothers, who had been transforming the Belgian textile industry since the last years of the eighteenth century, turned, after the war, to the production of the latest steam engines, pumps, hydraulic presses at their engineering works at Seraing— perhaps the greatest works of their kind in Europe—and boasted that they had all the latest inventions within ten days of their appearance in England. A young Westphalian locksmith was sent in 1819 by the Prussian government to learn the latest English methods of machine production; and as far away as Vienna the directors and foremen of cotton mills were chiefly British emigrants. Britain was already qualifying for the title of workshop of the world.

As an episode in economic history, the transition to industrialism in Britain has a special significance. It represents the classic example of self-generated take-off from a traditional, basically agricultural

[1] See T. S. Ashton, *An Economic History of England in the 18th Century*, p. 112, for the classic statement of the economics of the innovating process.

and commercial economy to sustained economic growth through specialization of processes, technological innovations—sometimes in alliance with scientific discoveries—and the exchange of a surplus of manufactured goods for food and raw materials in other parts of the world. It involved the community in a simultaneous creation of new forms of industry and transport and in an immense effort in agriculture and building to feed and house a new industrial population; and it placed new strains on a social and political system which had to reconcile the demand for increased output with the dawning awareness on the part of labour that industrialization held the key to economic advance for all and not only for the privileged few. The change was accomplished peacefully but not without periods of severe social stress owing to the fluctuating nature of the commercial system and the absence of effective means of dealing with the social consequences. Perhaps here lies the main weakness of the entire structure of the new industrial society; and any effort to strengthen it was imprisoned within the unyielding carapace of classical economic theory. To the two most influential minds of the day, the outlook was either gloomy or catastrophic: Ricardo feared that the relentless growth of population would lead to pressure upon the margin of cultivation, a prelude to inevitable stagnation of the economy; to Marx, the successive commercial crises with their social and political overtones were symptoms of underlying instability leading to collapse and revolution. Both were proved wrong. The continuous enclosure of new land for the new farming removed the danger of a relapse into over-population and under-investment that haunted Ricardo; and the successive triumphs of technology enabled the productive system to falsify the prophecies of Marx by providing a rate of growth of the national income that outstripped the growth of population. Whereas the population of Britain nearly quadrupled between 1801 and 1901, the national income increased eightfold, and *per capita* income which, in real terms, nearly doubled in the first half of the century, more than doubled again in the second half.

To contemporaries who watched, not without apprehension, the process of economic transformation taking place, the main agent of growth was the accumulation of capital, and the factors which favoured it were accorded a place of special importance. To Adam Smith (who took his stand in the pre-transition period) 'every prodigal appears to be a public enemy and every frugal man a public benefactor'; and to Ricardo, impressed—perhaps obsessed—with the rise in population, the continuous growth of capital and its embodiment in new forms of machinery were necessary for the maintenance of profits, rents, and wages alike. As we know now, Ricardo and his followers took an unnecessarily gloomy view of the prospects of industrial society, and many of their contemporaries refused to share it, but all agreed on the paramount need of capital accumulation and technical improvements and the necessity of removing obstacles that might interpose themselves between the productive process and the market or impede the efficient use of capital resources.

A particularly important role, therefore, fell to the man of business, the merchant or manufacturer or improving farmer and landlord—the entrepreneur as the economists called him—who undertook the work of directing capital resources to their alternative uses. It was mainly his own capital that he was directing, and he was usually responsible, along with his partners if he had any, to his last shilling for the debts of the firm in the event of failure. In return for the profits of enterprise, he set his own and sometimes other people's capital in motion by employing labour at subsistence wages and providing tools and materials with which they were enabled to supply the needs of the market. In the eyes of contemporary theorists, he was relatively a passive agent of market forces of which the consumer was king.

In the light of recent studies based on the records left by some of the pioneer firms, modern historians would accord the entrepreneur a wider and more human role, especially in the case of the large new firms which took the lead in the advance to machine production. Such firms broke new ground not merely in the application of technical innovations to existing processes, but through improvements in organization and management of labour and in the study of market forces. In regard to the study of the market, the tradition of quality established by the eighteenth-century pioneers was being challenged in the 1830s both in textiles and iron production owing to the greater attention given in France and Germany to standards of taste and quality, and it is worth noting that the most doctrinaire exponents of *laissez-faire* felt that here was a field in which British industry might well look to the State for assistance. Dr. John

Bowring of the Board of Trade, in his tour of France in 1836, was greatly impressed by the numerous schools of design, usually dating from the Old Régime, which he found there, and the Select Committee which was appointed on his return recommended the establishment of similar schools in industrial centres in England. The Board of Trade acted in anticipation of the report and obtained £1,500 from the Treasury for the opening of the first school of its kind consisting of two rooms in Somerset House in 1837; by 1843 there were six in different parts of the country representing the results of local initiative in alliance with the resources of the State. 'It would be by their excellence . . . combined with a moderate price', said one of the pioneers of this development, himself a manufacturer, 'that British goods would maintain their competitive position.'

Improvement in organization involved the early factory master in problems of recruitment and management for which the traditional system of putting-out through irresponsible middlemen was by no means the best preparation. Arkwright and Strutt, who initiated the revolution in cotton spinning, owed their success not only to their business acumen but to the imagination which they brought to the human problems of machine industry. They were community builders as well as organizers of production, and they and their successors, the Gregs of Styal, Benjamin Gott of Leeds, John Fielden of Todmorden, John Heathcoat of Tiverton, the Ashtons, Ashworths, Whiteheads of Cheshire or Lancashire, combined outstanding efficiency in the management of their concerns with a rudimentary system of welfare which has a place of importance in the history of labour relations. Robert Owen, the chief of the community builders, was the first to realize that output did not necessarily vary directly with the length of the working day, and that the appallingly long hours that were possible under the more flexible domestic system were not only inhuman but might be relatively unprofitable under conditions of factory production. Sir Robert Peel, the leading factory master of the day, who had already been instrumental in passing the Act of 1802 to regulate the hours of parish apprentices, joined forces with Owen to initiate the proceedings that culminated in the Acts of 1819-20; and under the leadership of these two highly successful manufacturers, the long-sustained effort of the State to curb the rapacity of the average factory master was launched.

About the same time, the economic problems of Birmingham, where small-scale business was the rule, gave rise to a school of economic and political speculation which was not without effects in its day and retains the interest of scholars down to the present time. Thomas Attwood, a remarkable member of a remarkable family of iron-masters and bankers, was a life-long advocate of planning for full employment by means of currency reform and controlled inflation. Though he failed to persuade his contemporaries to anticipate the employment policies of the welfare state, be made an important contribution to the political problems of the time through the formation of the Birmingham Political Union in 1828 which aimed at uniting middle and working classes in a campaign of political reform. 'It was not Grey or Althorp who carried it (the Act of 1832)', said Daniel O'Connell, 'but the brave and determined men of Birmingham'; Lord Durham thought Birmingham had saved the country from revolution; and its latest historian, Professor Briggs, has no difficulty in showing that 'it was never the insensate industrial town of Mumford's myth'.

Even the raw iron towns of South Wales, the creation of two generations of iron-masters among the hills of Merthyr Tydfil, reflected something more than the brute quest of material wealth. Richard and William Crawshay of Cyfarthfa were outstanding men by any standard. The latter inherited his father's gifts as well as his fortune, and showed capacities of statesmanship which made the gigantic concern of Cyfarthfa, it has recently been said, 'a beneficently stabilizing influence in the industry'.[1] His rival, Sir Josiah Guest of Dowlais, a devout Methodist, was an intimate of scientists and inventors, and provided Michael Faraday at the Royal Institution with samples of Dowlais iron for his studies in the qualities of hard and soft steel. Lady Charlotte Guest, mother of ten children and her husband's business associate, was a distinguished student of medieval Welsh literature and the first editor of the *Mabinogion*. The development of Middlesbrough and district under the influence of the remarkable Pease family, and the planned creation of Barrow-in-Furness by the Duke of Devonshire and his associates[2] are examples of forward looking vision as well as of the calculated pursuit of maximum returns.

[1] J. D. Evans, 'The Uncrowned Iron King', *The National Library of Wales* (7), 1951-2.
[2] See J. D. Marshall, *Furness and the Industrial Revolution* (1958), and below, p. 10.

The leading figures in the transition to machine industry (whatever may be said of the rank and file) cannot easily be fitted into the classical and Marxist mould of the capitalist inexorably confined by the cash nexus and mechanically adjusting himself to the movement of the market under the stimulus of marginal costs. Many industrial leaders could more easily be classified as products of religious dissent and perhaps, more particularly, of the superior education which dissenting schools provided. It is sufficient to refer to the part that the Quakers had played in the development of the iron industry, and their contribution to branches of science, medicine, and technology, entirely disproportionate to their numbers; to the work of industrial chemists trained in Scottish universities and English dissenting academies, to the stream of Scottish immigrants, particularly engineers, who brought their superior education and habits of application as the form of capital which was likely to yield the highest returns in the English revolution. The supreme self-confidence of the leaders of enterprise who were not only managers but the chief risk-takers of their concerns may have had its roots in the same source. They were acting in accordance with the character of a society in which the qualities of personal decision and responsibility were rooted in a long tradition of individualism in its most private and sacred aspects.

Not only the masters, but the men, especially in the new industrial communities of the North, the Midlands, and South Wales, were also coming under these influences. The sanctifying virtues of hard work, thrift, and self-denial were now being carried into the lives of the working classes themselves through a multitude of chapels and Sunday schools under the influence of the evangelical revival. These contributed also to the rise of effective working-class organization through the qualities of integrity and moral leadership which they evoked and on which durable trade unionism rested; and even the voices raised in indignant protest against the injustices and cruelties which industrialism brought in its train struck the authentic note of the age of self-discipline for moral as well as material ends. 'An idle man', said the redoubtable Parson Bull to the miners of Yorkshire, his neighbours and friends, '*is the devil's man*. Apply yourselves diligently to your calling—be not like some who *work hard* a few days, *drink hard* the rest—Three things then let me recommend—Religion as *the root*, and Industry and Patriotism as the *branches*.' Men and masters shared a common tradition and understood, if they did not always speak, a common language. The process of industrialization on which they were both engaged was a social as well as an economic process, and it reflected the energies of a whole people pursuing their material ends in a framework of values which accorded special importance to the qualities which could be turned to account in an age of unprecedented economic and social opportunities.

In agriculture the main emphasis of change was on the more efficient use of the land itself. To regard this change in land use as a mere undifferentiated drive towards enclosure for higher rents is to obscure its essential character. The introduction of the turnip and artificial grasses made possible the spread of arable cultivation of light soils that had hitherto lain idle; and while heavy soils were being put down to grass or cultivated in long leys for animal husbandry to satisfy the growing market for meat and particularly for tallow, lighter soils were being given over to mixed farming.

The special character of the British agrarian revolution—a revolution in land use involving appropriate advances in animal breeding and crop rotation—has important implications both on the side of capital formation and on that of labour supply. The English tenurial system, in accordance with which the landlord provided and usually maintained the fixed capital, implied a quasi-co-operative relationship between landlord and tenant which enabled the latter to retain a proportion of the profits of the joint investment and frequently encouraged the tenant to plough back his profits in improvements even though he might have no certain security of tenure or legal redress for loss of unexhausted improvements. The factor of confidence between landlord and tenant must be numbered among the imponderables that contributed to the process of capital formation in the period of transition.

Within the peculiar—and probably unique—context of the English agrarian system, the opportunities for saving were very wide. They were open not only to the owners of the soil but to a growing body of substantial tenant farmers; and the increasing volume of agricultural production fertilized intermediate areas of trading activities carried on by those involved in processing the raw materials of agriculture for milling, brewing, distilling, starch making, tallow chandling, and the like. A more direct impact of agricultural savings was made through rural and urban building and through the part which great landowners played, along with the great industrialists, in the development of transport, especially inland navigation.

Landowners were not slow to respond to the opportunities offered them in the nineteenth century. Their resources were greater than ever before, being swollen by urban rentals, although at the same time being burdened in some cases by unprecedented debts incurred in the course of patrician living. Few of the gentry of the north of England and the Midlands and South Wales failed to enlarge their incomes by means of leases of mineral rights, and some mined their own coal directly and even leased coal from others. Earl Fitzwilliam in Yorkshire, and the Earl of Crawford in Lancashire, managed their own enterprises; the Lowthers of Cumberland sank £500,000 in the mines, harbour, and general development of White-haven. They easily—indeed inevitably—passed from coal to rail-ways, and helped to promote companies that were likely to serve the needs of their own enterprises or enhance the value of their properties. (They could also obstruct development, and in other parts of the country railway companies often went out of their way to placate aristocratic opposition or to attract aristocratic invest-ment by reserving a proportion of the shares to landowners on the route of the railway: the reservation of one-third of the shares of the Liverpool and Manchester and one-fifth of the Great Western are two outstanding examples.) Lord Durham passed from railways to sea transport and marketed the products of his mineral empire in his own ships from the port of Sunderland; the Marquis of London-derry converted Seaham into a port and a steel town, and the seventh Duke of Devonshire took the lead, not only as chief risk-taker but as paramount managerial influence in the development of Barrow-in-Furness which grew from an isolated village of 150 inhabitants in 1846 to an industrial centre of 40,000 people in 1873, equipped with the largest and most efficient Bessemer steel plant in the world, a shipyard planned to employ 6,000 men, and a prosperous railway system which linked this previously unknown corner of England with the national railway network.

In the matter of agricultural investment, landlords differed widely: on the famous estates at Holkham the proportion of the rental invested in permanent improvement varied from 11 to 21 per cent. The Duke of Wellington—being a lavishly rewarded servant of the State as well as a model landlord—laid out nearly the whole of his rent on 'improvement of a stubborn soil'; most landlords were satisfied with an investment perhaps of 1 to 5 per cent of their gross rental for permanent improvement, and the net return after deducting overheads, taxation, repairs, etc., was only $2\frac{1}{2}$-3 or 4 per cent on improved land.

Powerful as the internal market was, it had also the reinforcement of a growing export trade to support the structure of machine industry. A population of less than twelve million people, according to the British census of 1801, was an insecure base for the transition to machine production; no more than 40 per cent of the output of the cotton industry, for instance, was absorbed by the home market in the first half of the nineteenth century; and it was fortunate—though not fortuitous—that the field of manufacture in which innovation had made its most spectacular advance coincided with the area of most elastic demand. Under the stimulus of rising wartime incomes and falling textile prices, the appetite for machine-made textiles grew with what it fed on, and, as a result of the invention of the cotton gin by Eli Whitney in 1793, the problem of supply was solved at a moment when shortage of raw material might have had disastrous results. From an average of 16 million lb. in the period 1783-7, the import of raw cotton rose to 28·9 million lb. in 1787-92 and 56 million lb. in 1800. At the same time, and in spite of wartime wages and prices, the price of cotton yarn showed a spectacular fall—from 38s. in 1786 for No. 100 yarn to 6s. 9d. in 1807.

An interdependent trading area was developed between Britain and the cotton states of the U.S.A. of the greatest importance to both, and, assisted by the monopoly enjoyed by British exports during the wars with France, the cotton industry pioneered the mass demand for British goods abroad. Between 1790 and 1815, after decades of stagnation, the volume of British exports to Europe nearly trebled and those to North America and the West Indies more than doubled, and for this, Professor Habakkuk has recently observed, Britain had to thank the vigilance of her fleets that kept the seas against her chief European rival as much as the inventiveness of British industrialists.

The role of the cotton manufacturer in the advance was phenomenal. By 1800 the proportion of cotton exports was 13 per cent of the total domestic exports; by 1806 it was 40 per cent; but whether we can regard the cotton industry as the leading sector in the British 'take-off', as claimed for it by Professor Rostow, is questionable.[1]

It owed its phenomenal rate of growth in the first half of the century, in part at least, to the existence of an almost inexhaustible supply of cheap labour; and for the same reason the victory of the factory over the handloom was painfully slow. The more successful entrepreneurs were those who ploughed back profits into new and better machinery while retaining their handloom section where and for so long as comparative costs encouraged them to do so. Its multiplying effect upon other industries was limited. In contrast with the iron industry it depended for its raw material upon foreign sources of supply, and the purchasing power generated by the workers of the industry was disproportionately small compared to the increase of output. In the second quarter of the nineteenth century its total production quadrupled and 'total incomes generated in Britain increased by 50 per cent, but the workers' wages barely rose at all'.[2] Its influence was not sufficiently powerful to initiate the 'take-off', but it captured the imagination of the time, and stood as the characteristic symbol of the British workshop for the admiration and example of all the world.

(ii) *Industrial Society and the Coming of Machine Industry*

This widening of commercial horizons both at home and abroad called for a reorganization of the structure of industry and an adaptation of the labour force on a radical scale; but both the variety of forms of organization and the length of time during which the adaptation took place were greater than is sometimes realized. Birmingham, which claimed, through the famous firm of Boulton and Watt, to provide the world with steam engines, required very few for its own manufacturing processes. Here the 'garret master', with a £100 capital and his traditional skill, was still the typical figure; the great factory at Soho remained a 'magni-

---

[1] See H. J. Habakkuk and Phyllis Deane, *The Take-off in Britain*, and W. W. Rostow (ed.), *Economics of Take-off into Sustained Growth* (1965).
[2] Phyllis Deane, *The First Industrial Revolution*.

ficent exception', and it was not until the last quarter of the nineteenth century that machinery was devised (or imported from
America) which could enable standardized factory production to
compete with the products of the myriad small masters who supplied the highly specialized products of the finished metal trades:
light arms, jewellery, sporting guns, japanned products, etc. In
Sheffield it was much the same with the making of scythes, sickles,
table knives, where craftsmen, as in Birmingham, worked for
middlemen except in times of bad trade when they launched out on
a desperate gamble on their own. The cheapness of the metal on
which they worked was such that unemployed journeymen would
sometimes establish themselves on credit as small masters and con-
trive to dispose of their product—often of the lowest quality—as
best they could 'through new and strange channels on the meanest
terms, for money, for stuff, for anything, for nothing'. The first
cutlery factory which embodied all processes from steel making to
the hafting of the knife appeared in 1832, but owing to the variety
of style and quality of the finished product, there was still room for
the little man, and the factory product remained the exception for
many years.

The extraction of the coal on which the national economy rested
was not only non-mechanized but, except in the northern coalfield,
continued to depend on small sub-contractors (butties in the
Midlands and West County) who engaged to get coal at an agreed
price and employed their own labour; the production of iron was
often undertaken in the west Midlands by 'overhands' with their
own gangs of day labourers; even in the highly organized cotton
spinning the operative spinner belonged to a higher order of
workers than his 'piercer' whom he employed at wages half his
own; the building of a locomotive might be sub-contracted to a
piece master who would employ his own craftsmen and these in
turn would employ and pay their own workmen. In the textile
industries, there was an army of hand workers who were as much
part of the 'great industry' as the factory workers themselves, though
more susceptible to the ebb and flow of its commercial mechanism.
There were probably half a million weavers[1] in 1830 working for
cotton, silk, woollen, and linen firms, and not less than 50,000
framework knitters usually working for middlemen and many of

[1] See J. H. Clapham, *An Economic History of Modern Britain*, vol. i, p. 179.

them for large firms operating through a system of departmental managers. Such forms of employment were not widely different from those of the factory except that the operatives had to provide or pay for their own fixed capital equipment, so absolving the employer from the burden of initial investment and subsequent overheads. In cotton, the firm of Horrocks had 700 spinners working in factories at Preston in 1830 but an army of out-workers numbering over 6,000; silk throwsters at Congleton might have half their men in factories and half out; in hosiery I. and R. Morley had 2,700 framework knitters and a host of seamers and finishers of all kinds and no factory at all until after 1860.

To define the conditions which produced factory production is not easy, but it may be said that concentration was most advanced where power machinery could be applied and where numerous delicate processes called for co-ordination under skilled supervision in order to capture or to extend a known area of the market. This was especially the case when finishing processes involving new techniques of dyeing and printing were brought together by the merchant with his eye on the market, or in the manufacture of glass, soap, pottery, paper, which depended on the direct application of chemical knowledge, and in the machine tool shops and the metal industries calling for large investment of fixed capital as well as specialized skill.

Important and indeed revolutionary as these processes were, the advance was not such as to affect directly more than a small proportion of the population. In 1834, the historian of the cotton industry, Edward Baines, estimated the workers in cotton mills at about 210,000–230,000; that is, one in every eighty of the population, less than one-third of the female domestic servants, and perhaps one-eighth of those engaged in agriculture. Apart from the handloom weavers and framework knitters who were on the fringes of the 'great industry', there were tens of thousands of tailors, shoemakers, metal workers, country blacksmiths, cobblers, carpenters, sewing women, and between three and four hundred thousand workers in the building trades, almost untouched by the new machinery. Many other local industries had been touched and turned to decay; the last iron furnace of Sussex expired in 1828; Suffolk and Essex had already lost their ancient cloth manufacture; Oxfordshire was losing its coarse velvet trade and Witney some of its trade in blankets; Cirencester, Frome, Shepton Mallet, Taunton their famous West of England cloth, and Exeter its light woollens. There were some 'poor remnants' at Barnstaple and Tiverton; Bradford-on-Avon was saved by the rubber industry and Stroud went over to machine production and was able to hold its own perhaps because it had army contracts for finest quality cloth for officers' uniforms with which Yorkshire could not compete. The eastern wing of the cloth industry was in still worse plight; there were probably 10,000 hand-looms at Norwich in 1820 but by 1840 there were few, and Norwich had to make a fresh start with semi-mechanical boot and shoe manufacturing and ready-made clothes.

The representative Englishman, it has been said, was still a countryman in 1831, and the representative workman was still a handicraftsman in a traditional workshop, working with traditional tools. In 1851, the distribution of the population had changed in favour of the townsman, but the representative Englishman was still far from being a worker directly employed in machine industry. The victory of the factory over the older forms of industrial organiza-tion was slow and it was not until the last decades of the century that it became the dominant form of organization in a majority of industries. In 1851, those employed in the principal non-mechanized categories comprised about five and a half million workers and out-numbered those in the mechanized industries (including coal) by three to one; and of the one and three quarter million in the mecha-nized groups, half a million were cotton workers. The most numerous group after agriculture were the domestic servants. In 1851, their number had risen to over a million and was still twice as large as the cotton workers. At 1,039,000 they were drawing nearer to the agricultural group which now numbered 1,790,000 and together these two groups numbered more than double those engaged in manufacturing and mining. When Britain was the un-disputed workshop of the world, the 'great industry' on which it was based actually employed 1·7 million out of a total British popula-tion of 21 million.

The relative numerical weakness of the 'great industry' empha-sizes its revolutionary character. In 1851, it absorbed less than one-quarter of the principal occupation groups, but it made an essential contribution to an economy which now had to provide for a population that had nearly trebled in the course of a hundred years. In 1751, the British population is thought to have been $7\frac{1}{2}$ million; in 1831, it was $16\frac{1}{2}$ million; by 1851, it had grown to 21 million. It was, also, by this time, a predominantly urban population; in 1831, the proportion of British people in towns of over 20,000 was one-quarter; within a generation the proportion had risen to a half and was rapidly growing. By 1851, the representative Englishman was becoming a townsman.

The British 'take-off' had involved, in its early stages, not only the mobilization of resources for industrial growth—machinery, transport, agricultural improvements, public utilities—but for fighting a twenty years' war with France. Investment on this gigantic scale could not be undertaken without a sacrifice of current consumption; it was impossible to have both guns and butter and at the same time to build the factories and farms that produced them. The transition from war to peace in 1815 which cut off government expenditure coincided with the end of a phase in long-term investment in agriculture and transport and imposed therefore a double strain. Moreover, between 1814 and 1817, 400,000 ex-service men sought re-entry to civil life and population was rising by more than 200,000 a year; there was a temporary collapse of the iron industry following the cessation of government orders; the export industries were facing the resistance of tariffs after a post-war spree of dumping of accumulated stocks. Surplus labour organized hunger marches and clamoured for the vote; political economists talked of the need to check population growth; a handful of merchants petitioned for free trade; George and Robert Stephenson wrestled with the problem of the locomotive, but they were baulked of success until 1829. If the engineers had reached their goal a generation earlier, the quota of misery might have been less. The logic of economic growth, with its disparity between the relentless growth of numbers and the sporadic advance of innovation, took its course. The astonishing resilience of cotton and iron and the flow of funds into harbour installations, gas, water, and other utilities, saved the situation, and the period 1815-30 ranks as one of the most troubled yet one of the most productive of the century. Still wider fluctuations were to follow; the first railway mania raised the boom of 1834-6 to record heights, but the accumulated miseries of the down swing made the period 1837-42 the most critical of the century, and there is some reason for thinking that the real national income per head in 1840 was lower than in 1830. Between 1840 and 1850 the 'industry state', to use Sir John Clapham's expression, began to experience the invigorating effects of a rapidly expanding railway network and of a fleet of iron ships of which a growing proportion consisted of iron screw steamers,[1] the fruits of long-term investment and innovation of a previous generation; the reform of the tariff and the reintroduction of the income tax in place of the heavy excise duties helped to stimulate the home and foreign markets; and the time was approaching when the British standard of living would be carried forward on a tide of exports which exchanged at a premium in terms of food, especially meat and dairy produce. The harvest of a mature economy was at last beginning to be gathered.

[1] See J. R. T. Hughes and Stanley Reiter, 'The First 1945 British Steamships', *The Journal of the American Statistical Association*, 53, 1958, p. 360: 'The general adoption of iron in steam-ship construction dates from the 1840's, a full decade earlier than the accepted estimates . . . the iron screw steamer was prominent in new British steamship construction from at least 1851.' See also G. S. Graham, 'The Ascendancy of the Sailing Ship 1880–85', *Econ. Hist. Rev.*, August 1956.

2

The Advance of Machine Industry and Transport

(i) *Engineering, Textiles, Heavy Industry*

ADAM SMITH in his *Wealth of Nations* used the example of a pin factory to demonstrate the prodigious increase in quantity which could be effected through division of labour. Perhaps because he thought the inference was self-evident, he omitted to add that it provided also an opportunity for an improvement in quality; not merely more pins, but pins of different lengths and strength, pins for every kind of occasion. As Mr. Charles Wilson has recently observed, 'It is misleading to consider the industrial revolution merely in terms of undifferentiated commodities called cotton or woollens or iron. Such treatment obscures the fundamental fact that the need to be met was for highly specific versions of such general categories.' The manufacture of textiles, glass, pottery, paper, the standardized products of the machine shops, the specialized products of the animal breeders provide many examples of the truth of this statement, but it is less easy to find support for it in the products of the heavy industries. Here British producers were working within a peculiarly favourable geographical environment—'a show-case of geological formations ringed about by the near sea'—in Sir John Clapham's vivid phrase, and could overwhelm competition by sheer cheapness, though qualitative differentiation was by no means absent.

Whatever the marginal differences between them, all the branches of industry which were in process of mechanical transformation in the late eighteenth century were responding to the influence exercised by the greatest social force of the age, the emergence of a rural and urban middle class with new wants and standards of taste, and the resources with which to satisfy them. The revolution in the production of textiles sprang from a demand for light fabrics stimulated, though not initiated, by commercial contacts with the East; and the mechanical means to meet the demand called not only for the ingenuity of skilled workmen on the look-out for a quick way to a fortune, but for scientists who were working in the tradition of Boyle and Newton. Behind the phenomenal success of Lancashire cotton and Yorkshire worsted lies an achievement in the mastery of mechanical bleaching, dyeing, and printing which more properly belongs to the history of applied science. The chief technical limitation that still remained was in the manufacture of the producing plant itself, and this was removed through the work of the mechanical engineers. The leaders, Bramah and Maudslay, were products of the ancient tradition of English craftsmanship of which the nursery was London; but a disproportionate number of their successors were Scotsmen:[1] John and George Rennie, designers of bridges, docks, canals, later of railways and machinery; William Fairbairn, founder of a famous machine shop at Manchester, and his brother Peter who founded another at Leeds; Henry Bell, builder of the first steamship, the *Comet*; David Napier who contributed to mechanical printing and became the founder of an engineering dynasty; William Murdoch and James Nasmyth, not to mention Thomas Telford and John Macadam. Many of them were pupils at the famous Maudslay workshop in Lambeth. They came down to England to finish their training and they made up for their lack of capital by a native endowment of character as well as of skill which reflected their Scottish background of poverty, piety, and learning. They remind us that the industrial revolution was a historical not a geographical event, and that if the British people had not willed the means they would never have attained the ends of a machine industry, whatever the blessings showered on them in the economy of Providence.

Some of the most important steps in the process of mechanization were taken as a response to the challenge of natural obstacles rather than as a result of the stimulus of natural resources. It was noticed by Arthur Young that Birmingham lacked an adequate water supply

[1] See Charles Wilson and William Reader, *Men and Machines: a History of D. Napier and Sons, Engineers 1808–1958.*

and that a surprising amount of work in that busy centre was done by hand without the aid of machinery; but Birmingham owed little to the gifts of nature and a great deal to the ingenuity and determination of its inhabitants; and it is perhaps not surprising that it was here, through the genius of Boulton and Watt, that the search for a prime-mover which could break through the limitations of the water-wheel and the Newcomen engine was pursued with such revolutionary effect. The double acting steam engine, with its 'parallel motion' device for transmitting power both ways (a device which Watt himself ranked as his greatest achievement) marks a recognized watershed in the evolution of mechanics, but it awaited the appearance of a new race of engineers before it could become a generalized instrument for the application of power to the operations of industry. 'How could we have a steam engine if we had no means of boring a fine cylinder or of turning a true piston, or of planing a valve face?' asked James Nasmyth. Henry Maudslay took the first important step in mechanizing the boring of cylinder and valves; and ten years of intensive work on the screw-cutting lathe, continued at intervals and at great expense until his death in 1835, provided a basis for the development of planing and milling machines, so that by 1840 most of the primary machine tools for mechanical engineering had taken their modern shape. His pupils went on to make further contributions to the age of scientific technology in which the control of minute quantities was used to achieve gigantic results: Nasmyth's steam hammer, designed in 1839 to forge the castings for Brunel's *Great Britain*, was so 'graduated as to descend with power only sufficient to break an eggshell', and Joseph Whitworth's measuring machine of 1834 was capable of 'comparing yard standards to the accuracy of one millionth of an inch'. By 1835 Andrew Ure reported that his fellow Scotsman William Fairbairn, in his machine shop at Manchester, could turn out an equipped mill for any price, trade, site, or motive power, and Henry Bessemer found that he could have different pieces of the same machinery made quite independently in Manchester, Glasgow, Liverpool, and London. Through the work of the engineers, skill and precision had been generalized and brought to the service of large-scale production and the mass market.

In one branch of industry, the transition to mechanized production took place independently of the new engineering and even

of the steam engine; and it is fitting that this last striking achievement of the age of the apprenticed craftsman can still be examined
in the region where its impact was most dramatic and complete, in
the village of Cromford and the busy industrial town of Belper.
These centres were already nearly half a century old in 1820, dating
from 1771 when Jedediah Strutt and Richard Arkwright began to
build that series of cotton mills along the Derwent which inaugurated the systematic development of factory production and
revolutionized the ancient industry of spinning. All but one of the
mills erected by the Strutts have given place to modern structures,
but an iron-framed fire-proof building, formerly the North Mill,
erected in 1804, still stands to give the authentic flavour of the
Strutt era; the stream which provided the power and now turns a
single turbine is still harnessed by the original dams, and the
hundreds of stone cottages built for the mill workers 150 years ago
are serving the same purpose today. In erecting their second series
of massive and by no means inelegant factories at the beginning of
the nineteenth century, the Strutts incorporated the most advanced
ideas of mill design: iron-framed building with hollow pot flooring
as an answer to the ever present danger of fire; a furnace for heating
the rooms, and a ventilator flue running through the successive
floors carrying 'pure air, warmed when necessary . . . at the rate of
upwards of 100 gallons per minute per person'.

The Strutts with their 1,500–1,600 workers at Belper and
Milford, not counting their factory at Derby, were the largest of
the country manufacturers, though Robert Owen came a close
second with a total labour force of 1,600–1,700 at his mill at New
Lanark; there were some large country colonies in Scotland and one
in Wales employing more than 800 and others between 250 and 500,
including Styal; but the number of 'cotton lords' was actually very
small compared to the host of petty employers with their scores of
workers. In 1816 when steam had begun to bring the industry into
towns there were only nine mills—six of them in Manchester—with
more than 600 workers but there were eighty-five with less than
200. Altogether the large firms accounted for 14,000 out of the
60,000 cotton factory operatives at that time, and they never failed
to draw a distinction between themselves and their smaller and less
reputable competitors.

The first great advance after the post-war readjustments occurred under the influence of the speculative mania of 1825. A number of firms built factories in anticipation of demand and these were only gradually filled with machinery during the years of slack trade after 1826. Many of the large spinning firms began also to instal power looms to ensure the more regular employment of their new spinning mills. They could thus pass the burden of surplus output in slack times to the large number of hand-loom weavers whom they kept supplied with yarn when trade was good. The factories, it was said, were 'for steady and permanent demand' and the hand-loom weavers were to take the first shock of the fluctuations of the market —the blindly shifting demand of the foreign consumer and the rise and fall of the home demand for cheap cloths in response to the fall and rise of the price of food. The continuous advance of technical progress was accompanied by a steady fall in prices and a narrowing of profit margins, and mill owners tried to meet the problem of falling profits by spreading their overheads over a larger volume of output. By 1833, excess capacity had been absorbed and the industry was ready for a new phase of growth.

It came as a result of a fall in agricultural prices, which in alliance with rising foreign demand stimulated an upward movement of industrial prices. New capital—frequently supplied by mushroom joint-stock banks—was attracted to the industry and productive capacity rose rapidly. According to a survey made by the factory inspectors early in 1835 the total horsepower of steam engines in the cotton mills in Lancashire was 20,302; a second survey three years later raised the figure to 29,551, and it may have been more. The manufacturers complained of a shortage of labour to man the new mills and the poor-law authorities were induced to undertake their ill-starred experiment in planned migration from over-populated eastern counties to meet the needs of the factory masters.[1]

Owing to the collapse of American prices in 1837, there was a fall in exports and in prices, but the effects of slow maturing railway investment at home enabled many manufacturers to switch their output to the home market; there was a recovery in exports in 1838 and then a further fall in 1839. This, coupled with a disastrous harvest, curtailed the market, but manufacturers found ways and means of keeping up output as an alternative to cutting production

[1] See below, p. 120.

in their expensive new mills. The fall in demand, both in the home and foreign market, continued in 1841-2 and only those firms which could cut costs still further by introducing labour saving devices could weather the storm. For the first time since 1826 the consumption of raw cotton declined, but such was the buoyancy of this remarkable industry that the total volume of production in the black years of 1841 and 1842 was still higher than at any time before 1840. This was only made possible by constant technical improvements: the use of longer mules, and 'double decker' mules to increase output per man, and especially the spread of the self-acting mule during the boom of 1835-6. There was also a rise in the proportion of women and children employed. In 1841 Leonard Horner computed that at that date 60 per cent of the workers in cotton factories were under 20; barely 20 per cent were over 30.

This concentration of competitive power lent added weight to the tendency towards geographical concentration. Only the strongest firms of the Midlands—the Strutts, Arkwrights, Hollins —could survive; those of Ireland succumbed and apart from a strong detachment in Clydesdale, the counties of Lancashire, Cheshire, and Derbyshire had a virtual monopoly of the cotton spinning and weaving. The recovery of 1842-5 saw a further rapid expansion; Leonard Horner reported that there were 524 new factories under construction in his division alone, and the great army of hand-loom weavers which twenty years earlier numbered a quarter of a million in cotton alone was down to 40,000 or 50,000 The industrial revolution may be said to have run its course in cotton.

In wool, the process of mechanization went forward under similar cyclical influences but more slowly. It also took transitional forms such, for instance, as the 'company mills' where the processes of scribbling, slubbing, and fulling were carried out in power factories owned co-operatively by groups of small domestic clothiers. In worsted, where merchants had become manufacturers in order to capture the growing trade in fine light fabrics, capital was concentrated in fewer hands than in wool, and the industry was dominated by large-scale merchant producers who ploughed back accumulated profits from the traditional putting-out system in preparation for the transition to factory production. In his illuminating study of the Black Dyke Mills, Mr. Sigsworth observes that something of the history of the new power mills that sprang up in the 1820s and 1830s can be inferred from their names: 'Providence'; 'Perseverance'; and from the names of some of the villages in these bleak uplands from which the domestic workers were gradually absorbed: Hunger Hill, Beggarington, Slave Row, Swamp.

It was in these villages that the seeds of the triumph of the West Riding over the Norfolk worsted industry were sown before coal or iron or even water-power came to their aid. For more than a decade before the first worsted mill was established in 1787, Yorkshire had at least equalled and probably surpassed East Anglia in the output of worsteds. It was the work, as Sir John Clapham has said, of merchant producers taking the lead in 'a pushing, hardworking locality, with some slight advantages, attacking the lower grades of an expanding industry'; and other agencies added their influence after the first steps to success had been taken. As in cotton, there was great prosperity in the middle thirties, and between 1835 and 1838 the number of mills of all kinds in wool grew by 30 per cent; in worsted the advance was still more striking owing to the introduction, in 1837, of cotton warps along with alpaca and mohair as well as wool, which enabled worsted products to compete with those of cotton in the market for light elegant fabrics. The change represents a 'new era in the history of the Bradford trade', and between 1835 and 1838 the number of worsted mills grew by 65 per cent. Both industries were severely hit by the depression of 1841-2, and unemployment in Leeds, Halifax, and Bradford was, if anything, worse than in Manchester. The market for woollens and worsteds was less elastic than for cottons, and since a higher proportion of the work in the case of wool was still performed in the hand-loom weavers' cottages, the burden could be shared with the outworkers and there was less incentive to keep output high by cost reducing innovations. The number of power looms grew from just over 2,000 in 1835 to just under 10,000 in 1850, but there was still 'an abundance' of woollen hand-loom weavers in the second half of the century, probably as many—120,000—outside the factories as inside. The number in worsted was incomparably fewer; only wool-combing remained unmechanized, and in 1845 this last outpost of the handworker succumbed, with disastrous suddenness, to the work of the redoubtable Samuel Cunliffe Lister, merchant, inventor, and monopolist of wool-combing patents, and a large number of hand combers found themselves unwanted in a world already reeling from the collapse of the railway boom. The geographical concentration was also less pronounced in wool than in cotton; 40–50 per cent in the West Riding with 12 per cent still in the West Country. Worsted was the most concentrated of all, with 95 per cent in the West Riding and a mere remnant in Norfolk where it once dominated.

Subsequent change was in the direction of increased production through more completely automatic machinery. Between the 1840s and 1880s the size of cotton factories changed little but the output of yarn per operative doubled; in weaving the output per man rose nearly two and a half times while prices tended to rise. During the years 1849–61, 'the halcyon decade' as it has been called by the most recent historian of the industry, capital investment rose by over 60 per cent and looms by over 50 per cent and the importation of labour had to be organized by the leading firms from the eastern counties and even from Ireland. The Crimean War and the commercial crisis of 1857 temporarily checked the rate of growth, but the impulse given by the limited liability acts carried forward the wave of new investment until it was checked by the Cotton Famine caused by the American Civil War, only to be resumed with greater force when this was over.

A feature of the advance in cotton was the rise of co-operative joint-stock spinning companies in which the shares were owned by the operatives. Of the fifty which existed in 1863 with a capital of £2 m. apparently only eight survived in 1866—'a bitter experience to working men whose shares were totally unsaleable'. By far the most important was the Oldham Building and Manufacturing Company established in 1858—'not a co-operative society', said Mr. Gladstone, 'but an association of small capitalists employing other working men', and the model for all the succeeding 'Oldham Limiteds'. The great Oldham boom reached its height between 1873 and 1875 when thirty-three new co-operative limited companies were formed. Their methods were unorthodox; 'they were not intended to be models of soundly depreciated business units but rather to supply shareholders with dividends'; and the manner in which dissatisfied shareholders ousted boards of directors which failed to produce an acceptable balance sheet was thought 'comparable only to the attitude of the French revolutionaries to their unsuccessful generals'; but they built model mills, treated their workmen well, and made Oldham the greatest mill town in the world. Their success was due to the vigilance of shareholders, their pride in their mills, and their hunger for dividends; they enjoyed a longevity twice that of ordinary firms, and by the stimulus of their example they promoted efficiency throughout the industry.

The advance of 'Oldham Limiteds' in the middle 1870s was part of a general expansion of the cotton industry. Between 1873 and 1883 three hundred and seventy-three new cotton companies were floated and complaints of chronic overproduction began to be heard. A falling rate of profit was accepted as the only alternative to closing the mills; but drastic cost-reducing economies and a vigorous search for new markets in China, Asia, and Africa maintained the export trade at a satisfactory level, and in 1886 after more than a decade of the so-called Great Depression it was said, 'There is scarcely a nook or a corner in the habitable globe where the products of the spindles and looms of Lancashire do not find a market —while in respect of the business done with the open (non-protected) markets of the world, Manchester almost monopolizes the trade in cotton goods.'

In regard to worsted, the Lancashire cotton famine opened an opportunity to the mixed fabrics section which it took with both hands. Scorning mock modesty, Bradford proudly announced in 1862 that 'in plain mohairs, alpacas, lustres, orleans, coburgs in all colours, we cannot be equalled by the whole world in make, dyes, and finish, even though foreign manufacturers buy our own yarn and compete with us in these articles'. Owing to the cotton famine, wool prices were lower than those of cotton, and fashion began to swing back to all-wool worsteds in which French manufacturers held the lead. The threat from France was postponed by the Franco-Prussian war and Bradford was given another opportunity to profit by the misfortunes of others. By 1874, however, those complex symptoms which afflicted so many industries at the time began to show themselves in the familiar form of falling prices and profits and rising bankruptcies side by side with increasing consumption of raw material, new investment, and the employment of more workers. The competition of French all-wool worsteds again became the subject of complaint, and the shortcomings of British

spinning, dyeing, and designing and also of British technical education came under fire. The rise of tariffs against British goods turned
the attention of manufacturers to the formation of employers'
associations and the development of trade with the unprotected
markets of the world; but the 'soundless and immense development
of the home trade' under the influence of rising real wages was the
main factor in enabling expansion to take place, though at a
slower rate.

In hosiery, machine production had never penetrated although a
model of a circular frame which pointed the way had been invented
by Brunel in 1815. The very large firms like I. and R. Morley looked
with disfavour on the factory; they had their settled market in the
form of Court or army orders and had no incentive to change; the
workers regarded the factory as a form of slavery and preferred
the 'freedom' of their domestic workshops. The smallest firms of all
which dealt at cut-throat prices through bagmen—'a reptile race
who have wriggled themselves into the business'—and the independent owner of frames who lived by hiring them out to starving
stockingers, were also critical of the factory. The intermediate
firms which lacked the security of Court or War Office trade began
to find their position intolerable owing to the pressure of German
competition, and experiments began to be made in factory production. One of the earliest and certainly the most successful was the
firm of Hine and Mundella which established a power-driven
factory employing German machines to make tubular hose in 1851.
By taking up the innovations of ingenious workmen, Mundella
quickly went on to produce fully fashioned hose, and, along with
other firms which followed his example, stimulated the hosiery
industry to such effect that the displaced workers were quickly
absorbed by the expansion of the finishing processes, and the
expected crisis of technological unemployment failed to materialize.
The unprecedented prosperity which followed was only broken
with the general price fall in the middle 1870s. A persistent depression now settled on the industry, a depression of prices and profits
which was attributed to cut-throat competition of many small
firms, the resistance of trade unions to wage cuts, and the impact of
German competition. More discerning critics pointed also to the
technical backwardness of even the best English artisans who were
totally lacking in the knowledge of machine drawing and designing

and in the chemistry needed for the dyeing and finishing trades. In Germany, it was said, technical education could be obtained 'on the spot at a cost of as many shillings as it requires pounds in England'; and British merchants were criticized for lack of selling enterprise. There was heavy mortality among small firms unable to make the economies required for the new competitive conditions, but large firms under enterprising management went on from strength to strength and established a dominating position in the industry.

In the history of the 'great industries' the key to commercial advance was the introduction of technical innovation for the purpose of capturing progressively wider sections of the market by reduction of price relatively to quality. The only important exception to this rule was the coal industry. Such qualitative differentiation as there was—steam coal, different qualities of domestic coal—was the work of nature not of man, and the extraction of coal conforms more closely than manufacturing forms of industry to the conception of the industrial revolution as a blind struggle for undifferentiated quantity production. Owing to a record rate of natural increase, supplemented by migration from overpopulated Welsh villages, labour supply in the mining communities kept pace with demand, and the advance of machinery was slow. The steam engine affected only the surface machinery—pumping, winding, ventilation; the actual getting of the coal remained the work of miners with pick and shovel and gunpowder. The attention of entrepreneurs was concentrated on the problem of transport from the pit face to the pit top, and the substitution of mineral fuel for organic fuel, with all its attendant consequences, proceeded on the basis of cheap labour for winning it and sophisticated technology for moving it.[1] By the 1830s the deep pits of Tyneside were beginning to adopt the two-decker metal cage running on iron guide-rods for the winding of coal and men, and by the 1840s the wire rope was being fitted to the more powerful winding engines in the more progressive collieries. Elsewhere, miners hung free with a leg through a rope-loop on the cable. The only mitigation of the miners' physical labour had come as a result of the use of wheeled trams at the end of

[1] See E. A. Wrigley, 'The Supply of Raw Materials in the Industrial Revolution', *Econ. Hist. Rev.*, August 1962.

the eighteenth century on light rails of iron, and by 1840 the endless rope haulage system operated by stationary engines along the main roads was just coming in; but human muscle—male and, until 1842, female in some pits—remained the prime mover along the subsidiary roads and even up the shaft itself in the more backward pits.

The hazards of working increased with the deepening of the underground workings, and the dreaded fire-damp or methane gas exhaling from the coal seams took an appalling toll. The impotence of ingenuity, however heroic, against the forces of nature was never more poignantly shown than in the successive efforts of miners to overcome these hazards: the flint and steel mill; the reflection of light from the surface of mirrors; even the phosphorescent glow of decaying fish. George Stephenson and W. R. Clannie were already at work on the problem, but in 1813 the most eminent scientist of the day, Humphry Davy, was intercepted on his return from a shooting trip in the Highlands by an anxious clergyman with an urgent request to bring his scientific knowledge to the aid of the miners of the Wear and Tyne, and within three weeks the principle of the gauze-protected light was triumphantly demonstrated. No further contribution was made by the scientists until 1845 when Faraday—the only scientist of distinction to pay disinterested attention to the problems of industrial technology—hinted at the part played by dry coal dust in colliery explosions (an observation which was of importance in connexion with the mysterious series of explosions in coal-burning ships at sea) but it went unregarded.

Mining engineers failed to improve upon the hazardous method of creating an air current by means of a furnace in the up-shaft, but mines continued to get deeper and more dangerous. After a series of terrible disasters between 1845 and 1850 the air pump and fan already in use in the deep French and Belgian pits were introduced into the fiery pits of South Wales and slowly made their way through the British coalfields; a more important consequence was the Act of 1850 which made the appointment of a technical inspectorate a statutory obligation and led in the following years to an understanding of the scientific basis of mine ventilation; but it was left to Robert Galloway, mining engineer and first historian of the industry, to provide positive proof that dry coal dust was the most potent source of colliery explosions.

The biggest source of coal supply was the ancient northern field of the Wear and Tyne, which in the 1830s and 1840s yielded probably a quarter of the total production of Britain. The pits were deep, 1,000 feet or more, and the most fully organized in the country, each employing hundreds of men and representing an investment of £240,000 to £500,000 of capital. Engineering skill was at its highest in these pits, and so were the dangers which grew with the increasing depth and ramifications of the underground workings.

As the railways spread into the hinterland of the rivers, more and more pits were sunk, usually by partnerships of capitalists who took out fractional shares in the concern. In the boom of 1836–7 two joint-stock companies, each of £500,000 capital, were launched, but the outcome did not encourage the supersession of the old partnership system. Of the other main fields, that of Lancashire probably came second in output; Staffordshire had the deepest pit of all, 2,100 feet, but also many shallow pits with immensely thick seams, in some cases, mere quarries on the sides of hills. Shallow workings and surface pits predominated in Wales, Yorkshire, Cumberland, and Scotland, and in the Forest of Dean, and in Somerset there were pits which were mere well-holes measuring only four or five feet across. From an approximate 10 million tons in 1800, the output of British mines rose to 44 million tons in 1850, and, under the gigantic stimulus of the thirty years of prosperity which followed, to 154 million tons in 1880.

The impact of this flood of heat and energy was felt far beyond the market which it served at home; coal became an essential factor in the nation's trade and, through the work of the British mercantile marine, in world trade. From less than half a million tons in 1831 (when the export duty was removed), the export trade rose to $1\frac{1}{2}$ million tons in 1841 and to 8 million tons in 1861. British coal was in such demand, said Stanley Jevons, in his paean to King Coal, that it dictated the price to native fuels in nearly all the maritime parts of the world. This was due not only to its quality but to the fact that outgoing ships carrying cargoes of higher value but of less bulk than incoming ships with their cargoes of food and raw materials, took coal as ballast, even to the eastern ports of America. British tramp steamers could do business along the sea lanes in the comfortable knowledge that they could adjust the price of their ballast coal according to local circumstances and rely on the rates of back-carriage for their main profit.

Professor Jevons was troubled by such feverish consumption of the national reserves of power, and in 1867 he wrote, 'In the increasing depth and difficulty of coal mining we shall meet that vague but inevitable boundary that will stop our progress. We shall begin as it were to see the furthest shore of our Black Indies. The wave of population will break upon that shore and roll back upon itself.' This gloomy forecast was quickly forgotten in the boom of the early 1870s; an immense expansion of world demand for iron, especially railway iron, caused a sharp rise in the price of coal and this was answered between 1871 and 1875 by the opening of more than 1,000 new pits. The iron industry, which consumed one-third of British coal output, and was very sensitive as to its price, introduced important cost-reducing innovations and the consumption of fuel was drastically cut. When the boom broke in 1873, there was competition among coal producers to dispose of surplus stocks and a sharp fall of prices and profits, and a loss by the miners of a large part of the gains they had extorted during the boom years. Output continued to rise but more slowly, to meet the expanding world demand, and the low price of British coal was an important factor in the successful transition of the iron industry to the age of steel and to the advance of industrialization in parts of the world where alternative supplies were lacking or less accessible.

As early as 1767 a Swedish traveller commented on the energy with which Anthony Bacon, the iron king of Cyfarthfa, and the Homfrays of Penydaren were attacking the problem of applying coal to the production of wrought iron, and asked 'if there is not after all some reason to dread the injury to our iron trade with which the people of this country frighten us'. Visitors came from the U.S.A. and Europe, including the redoubtable Alfred Krupp, who stayed in the country under an assumed name and learned all that the steel workers of Sheffield could teach him. The Seven Years War had fathered many new furnaces, including Carron in Scotland and Dowlais in Wales. During the Napoleonic War the productive capacity of the industry quadrupled. There were the giants like Carron, described as the arsenal of Europe, and Cyfarthfa, now under the masterful control of William Crawshay, with their thousands of employees; there were concerns in Yorkshire, Wales, and the west Midlands employing between 700 and 1,500; and a very large number below this figure, down to pygmy concerns of half a dozen men. In 1814 the average size in the whole of Scotland was twenty. In Staffordshire, where, it was said, property was so divided that there was a coal mine to every field, there were many concerns of middling size with a capital of £5,000 subscribed by local tradesmen and bankers and often depending on their tommy shops to keep them afloat.

With peace came a price fall and acute competition in foreign markets from Sweden and America. The demands of peace, however, soon out-stripped those of war and, under the stimulus of the 1825 boom, output rose to almost double the wartime record. The new iron age had arrived—the age of iron rails, iron pipes, iron bridges and boats, iron churches and chapels; the Prime Minister, Lord Liverpool, even spoke of iron pavements to stimulate demand in the slack post-war years.

Output dipped in the dull years 1829-32 and a new threat to the leadership of the English iron-masters came as a result of the work of James Neilson, manager of the Glasgow Gas Works. He qualified for his post by attending evening classes in science at the Andersonian Institute at Glasgow—probably under Professor Andrew Ure—and tested his theories by studying the effect of heated air on the combustion of coal-gas. In 1829 he persuaded the Clyde Iron Works to give his hot blast a trial, and by doing so effected a minor revolution in the industry. The black band ironstone which David Mushet and other Scottish iron-masters had been vainly trying to subdue since 1802 was now brought into the market with a headlong impetus which astonished and alarmed their southern neighbours. From 37,000 tons in 1830, Scottish output rose to 147,500 in 1841 and 547,000 in 1847—more than a quarter of the whole British make. Fortunately for the iron-masters south of the border, their puddling techniques were superior to those of Scotland and the railway iron of the English and Welsh furnaces had no peer. An American agent who is said to have placed an order for 40,000 tons in 1835 wrote that 'All countries throughout the world must get their railway iron in England where it is manufactured so rapidly and so perfectly that it is useless to pretend to compete with this branch of industry.' The English and Welsh iron-masters also tried to blunt the edge of competition amongst themselves by price agreements in 1831-2,

1837, 1840, and at other times; but they either lacked the will or the means to keep them.

The demand for railway iron fell off in 1841, and the domestic market was hit by the general depression of 1841-2. *The Times* of December 1841 placed the blame on the Scottish iron-masters; they had deluged every part of Britain, it said, with their product; prices had been forced down even in Scotland below the cost of production, 'the workmen in the meantime being ground down to the earth to enable the masters there to continue their insane conflict with each other as to who should produce the greatest quantity at the lowest level'. For the first time, all regions were affected; in some districts half the blast furnaces were out of action and total production fell by 28 per cent.

In 1843 it began to climb and by 1845 the output was again at a record height and still climbing; by 1847 it topped two million tons, mainly for the lengthening railway network at home and abroad. Railway lines were not only getting longer, they were also getting heavier owing to the increasing weight of rolling stock; and until 1844, Britain had no competitor in the United States where facilities for making heavy iron rails did not yet exist.

By 1847 the railway boom was over; there were wage cuts, unemployment, strikes, and panic selling by the weaker producers; 62 per cent of South Staffordshire furnaces were out of blast; 31 per cent of those of Scotland and 22 per cent of those of Wales. But severe though the crisis was, its effect on output was rather to check growth than to induce a net decline, and by 1849 the upward climb was resumed. There was a slight but significant shift in direction. The Scottish share of the national production which had reached about 28 per cent in 1850 began to go down and by 1880 it was less than 14 per cent. Staffordshire which had claimed 30 per cent in 1850 sank to 8 per cent; Wales from 25 to 12 per cent. Cumberland and Lancashire rose from insignificance to 20 per cent, and Northumberland and Durham from 5 per cent to over 30 per cent. The immediate future lay with Middlesbrough, not only by reason of the iron resources of the Cleveland Hills, but also because Bolckow Vaughan and Co. took the opportunity of their late arrival to introduce the latest methods—particularly the use of waste gases—and the largest furnaces. The Middlesbrough methods of larger and hotter furnaces spread to the new smelting districts of Barrow and north Lincolnshire. In 1855 the total British make of pig-iron was over three million tons; in 1870 it was over six million, and the greatest boom of the century was round the corner. Between 1866 and 1872 exports doubled—from 1·7 to 3·4 million tons of which railway iron represented nearly one-third. Half went to the U.S.A.; 13 per cent to Russia. The best customer for pig-iron was Germany. Altogether, more than half the exports went to iron producing countries, a situation that could only be temporary. Thirty new furnaces were built in Cleveland between 1869 and 1874, adding more than 50 per cent to its producing power. From world boom to world slump was only a matter of months. In 1876 iron exports were down by more than one-third mainly owing to the collapse of the German and American markets; there was also a shift from iron to steel; by 1876 the trade in iron rails was said to be 'dead' and by 1879 twenty out of forty-four Cleveland firms were bankrupt. But the demand for shipping iron rose as that for railway iron declined, and the total output made a sharp recovery at a drastically lower level of price.

Competition was now internal as well as external, as a result of the coming of cheap steel. It was twenty years since Bessemer had read his famous paper with the paradoxical title 'The Manufacture of Iron without Fuel' at the meeting of the British Association at Cheltenham in 1856. But the way of the innovator was far from smooth. As is well known, he 'forgot the phosphorus', his licensees gave up in disgust, but after three years' further experiment he established his own firm in Sheffield and forced his process on the industry by underselling his competitors while at the same time making fabulous profits. Siemens's open hearth process also found little favour with existing firms, and the inventor had to form his own company at Swansea in 1869 to begin the marketing of his product. In the case of Gilchrist Thomas, who solved the problem of the phosphoric ores, the final step into production was made possible when the Bolckow Vaughan works at Middlesbrough placed themselves at the disposal of the inventor in 1879, and opened a new era in the metallurgical industries of Britain and the world.

The cool welcome which iron-masters gave to cheap steel sprang partly from their ingrained conservatism and suspicion of scientific as distinct from traditional methods, and also from the fact that the process of making basic steel was better adapted to the ores of the Continent, especially the minette ores, than to those of Britain. The challenge to British iron-masters was intrinsically more serious than to their competitors abroad and they were technically less well equipped to meet it.

The struggle for foreign markets after 1873 called for drastic economies; fuel consumption in iron manufacture was cut by one-third and labour costs on a ton of steel rails were said to be cut by half. Between 1873 and 1883 the price of iron and steel rails fell by 60 per cent. Iron-masters were responding to the challenge in other ways. 'Twenty years ago', said William Siemens in 1886, 'I certainly found the greatest possible difficulty in getting iron-masters to look at new ideas, but since that time the Iron and Steel Institute has been founded and men who formerly ridiculed the idea of chemical analysis now speak of fractional percentages of phosphorus and sulphur with respect.' New demands were being made upon the skill and enterprise of the British iron and steel industrialists if they were to maintain their place beside competitors even more richly endowed than themselves. A measure of their achievement is provided by the figures of exports of iron, steel, and machinery, which, after falling in 1878 to 3 million tons, rose in 1882 to 5·6 million tons, an advance of more than 40 per cent on the boom year of 1873.[1]

(ii) *Railways, Shipping, Scientific Technology*

In the form of private mineral lines, linking up coal mines with waterways, railways had long been a familiar feature of the industrial landscape. In the early nineteenth century they began to be equipped with primitive forms of locomotives, and in 1825 steam locomotion was authorized for the first time on a public railway—the Stockton and Darlington. How far it was from representing a challenge to the canal or even to the horse may be seen in the Report of the Directors in 1827 when they gloomily estimated that the use of the locomotive represented a saving of less than 30 per cent over horse-haulage—'and that', as a disgusted inquirer wrote, 'on a line to carry coals where fuel costs were negligible'. The horse and the canal seemed safe enough, but in fact the doom of both as primary factors in the national transport system was being sealed as the

[1] See W. W. Rostow, *British Economy of the Nineteenth Century*, p. 72.

result of two important technical innovations. In 1820 John Birkinshaw, the foreman of the Bedlington iron works, took out a patent for the wrought iron edge rail which superseded the clumsy and brittle cast iron flange rail and so solved the problem of the permanent way; in October 1829, the directors of the Liverpool Manchester Railway, divided as to the comparative merits of stationary and locomotive engines, held the famous trials at Rainhill which ended in the overwhelming triumph of George and Robert Stephenson's Rocket.

The monopoly of the local waterways was now at an end, a doom for which they themselves were partially responsible. Through their control of the Trent and Mersey canal and their ownership of warehouses at the terminus, they had been able to impose their own terms on the users of the canal, so that goods sometimes piled up for six months and mills stopped work for lack of transport. The permanent way and the steam locomotive had arrived, and joint-stock capital proceeded to build the first instalment of the railway network. By 1838 five hundred miles of railway were in operation; by 1843 the mileage had risen to 1,900 and by 1848 to 4,600; nearly 1,000 miles of canals were bought or leased by the railways but 2,750 miles of independent canal remained to compete for the traffic in heavy goods.

The Liverpool and Manchester had, in fact, inaugurated the railway age; it was undertaken before the problem of traction had been solved and in a period of depression, and represents a triumph for the courage and foresight of the group of solid, largely Quaker, capitalists who promoted it. Henceforth, capital was easily—sometimes too easily—mobilized; an advertisement in a railway magazine was sufficient in time of boom to invite a flood of applications without the necessity of calling on the machinery of the money market, and stockbrokers played a secondary role; main-line companies usually supported branch-line flotations and amalgamations often merely formalized already existing arrangements. Railways were self-stimulating; cheap and speedy traffic created more traffic; latent wants became active; dormant demands clamoured to be met; feeder lines were demanded by towns in the neighbourhood of the main line and the grasping of opportunity by one interested party facilitated the fulfilment of the ambition of another. These consequences flowed mainly from the profound and varied effects the railway had upon the market: of lowering the cost of raw materials, especially heavy materials; of increasing the market area in which goods could be sold, especially perishable goods of the dairy and the garden; of narrowing the distance between producer and consumer and so encouraging him to operate on a larger scale; of breaking down local monopolies, e.g. the Wear and Tyne Coal Vend and the canal companies; of creating entirely new markets, e.g. for railway accessories for swift and comfortable travel, such as rubber buffers.

Socially, they exercised a levelling influence since trains carried members of all classes, and they tended to unify the nation through swifter posts, national newspapers, and the growth of holiday traffic. There were gains for poor and rich and for most parts of the country. Until the railways came, coal was an unobtainable luxury to the poor of East Anglia and a tax on the declining Norfolk industries; and a Norfolk farmer told James Caird that the railway saved him £600 per annum which had formerly been incurred in driving his fat stock to the London market, a journey which lasted 12–14 days and reduced the weight of his bullocks by 28 lb. and his sheep by 7 lb. The railways helped in the revival of Norwich and assisted grain farmers to meet the challenge of free trade; they stimulated the iron, coal, and engineering industries to new and unprecedented levels of production; they also served as a stabilizing force during the critical years 1846–8 when it is calculated that they gave employment, directly, to a quarter of a million men; and in the subsequent period of steady expansion culminating by 1880 in a network of 16,000 miles, they created not only a nation-wide service of swift and punctual transport but a new industry which was to play an important part in the world of organized labour.

While the gain to the community in economic terms was incalculable, the prizes of speculation were distributed with impartial injustice among those who carried the risk. They risked their savings and frequently sacrificed their income for the promotion of projects that secured the most rapid rates of growth in the expectation that they would also yield the highest rates of profit; but in view of the many abortive enterprises, of the shameless exploitation of railway promotions by landlords and lawyers and also by local authorities who regarded them as milch cows for the extraction of local rates, it is by no means certain that the expectation was realized. The victims and the prize-winners were drawn from a surprisingly wide social range, and included, according to *The Times*, many parsons who forsook their scripture for their 'scrip', a tribute to the resources of the Victorian clergy as well as to the repute of railway shares.

The choice of railways as the outlet for savings in the boom of 1844 was inevitable; of all the joint-stock promotions of 1835-6 railways had proved the most stable; several, e.g. the London–Birmingham and the Liverpool–Manchester, were returning 10 per cent; a number of others 6 per cent or more. By 1844 railways were both respectable and profitable. Moreover they had been instrumental in developing provincial share markets to which provincial capital and perhaps especially Lancashire capital was attracted. Manchester, Liverpool, Glasgow, Leeds, Wakefield, Bradford, Halifax, Huddersfield, Leicester, Birmingham, indeed (it was said) every town of 10,000 to 20,000 inhabitants had its share market. Railways were in a peculiarly strong position not only to tap but to drain these resources of capital. Unlike most other forms of investment, railways had to be completed in almost every detail before they could begin to earn revenue; the ultimate purchaser of railway shares had therefore to see the project through—even though it took from two to five years—or lose his capital altogether.

This characteristic of railway investment became a source of anxiety to individuals and of embarrassment to the economy as a result of the mania of 1844-5, and the question of how the capital (a total of £150 m. between 1846 and 1850) was to be found for completing the projects became urgent. Promoters flooded the Board of Trade with schemes of incorporation; investors scrambled for shares and speculators led them on by offering provisional shares in the form of 'scrip' which was subsequently exchanged against partially paid up certificates. If the 'scrip' was issued to 'Bearer' it could be used as a negotiable instrument and presented as security for further speculation. When calls were made on 'scrip', as on unpaid share certificates, the holder might find that he had overreached himself, and the fact that the liability was 'limited' did not in such cases prevent him from losing his all. When the prices of stocks began to fall in the autumn of 1845, £30 m. of share capital in joint-stock companies was lost in three weeks, and between 1845 and 1847 the shares of ten leading railway companies fell by £78 m.

In the subsequent inquiry, it was found that dividends had been frequently paid out of capital in order to attract more capital; that stock holders were receiving interest before the project had begun to earn dividends and on holdings that were not fully paid up; that many had been tempted to assume liabilities beyond their means. There were insistent demands for government audit of railway accounts but the railway interests which had a large voting strength in parliament, in alliance with those who had a rooted fear of government interference, killed a Bill introduced in 1849 for that purpose. There were other aspects of railway development which were more successful in securing public supervision. In 1842 the Board of Trade was empowered to ask for returns of traffic and of accidents. In 1844 the State acquired the power to revise rates and even to purchase new lines, and the Parliamentary train provided a daily return train at 1d. a mile for third-class passengers. It marked a tardy recognition that third-class passengers were a much neglected source of revenue and were worthy of being treated as human beings rather than as inanimate freight. The committee of 1846 looked into the appalling conditions of the 200,000 navvies and made far-reaching recommendations (including the recognition of workmen's compensation as a responsibility of the companies), which were in advance of the time but were not without good effects especially in regard to the worst evils of truck. In 1850 the Clearing House—'a sort of Federal Council of the English railway companies'—organized to arrange through-rates for goods and passengers using different lines, was incorporated by Act of Parliament, and gave an impetus to the movements for amalgamation of companies into larger units. The Commission of 1872, appointed to report on the dangerous tendency to monopoly, could only report that the merging of railways had maintained the advantages while reducing the evils of chaotic competition. At the same time, the struggle between companies to capture the traffic led to the building of feeder lines with an eye especially to the traffic in heavy freight such as coal and iron which had been the monopoly of the canals. Successive inquiries undertaken by anxious legislators had to confess that the steady progress of this new monster of railways towards monopoly was not incompatible with an enormous acceleration of internal trade at rates over which the State could exercise no effective control. Railway rates were a legacy of nearly a thousand railway

Acts and constituted a legalized chaos through which only the railways themselves could find a tortuous way. In 1873 the Railway and Canal Commission was appointed to hear complaints and to decide on the reasonableness of through-rates; it also had authority to examine, and if necessary to kill, proposals for further amalgamations and the purchase of canals. Perhaps the warning was taken too much to heart; the acquisition of canals ceased and the waterways of England have remained in a state of suspended animation from that day. The opportunity of integrating them into a national system of transport was lost.

There were other, and in a social sense, less expendable victims than canals. The country markets living by horse-drawn and hoofborne traffic dwindled; coastal and river towns were sometimes stimulated but more often withered by the touch of railways; the ports of London, Liverpool, Hull, Glasgow were great railway termini and sucked the traffic from the regional centres of inland and coastal trade. The coal trade of Lynn, Boston, and Wisbech was captured by the railways; the little ports of north Norfolk were hamstrung by interior railway lines; many historic ports of southern and western England, of Wales and Scotland declined, and even Bristol fell back in the race with the ports serving great industrial hinterlands. On the other hand, some new ports sprang to the front; above all Southampton and Cardiff; holiday traffic brought a new kind of life to some old ports and turned seaside villages into centres of the holiday industry.

The railways were an industry as well as a service. They employed 65,000 male workers in 1851 and 174,000 in 1881, many of them living in the new towns such as Crewe and Swindon built expressly for them by the railway companies. The deadly monotony of these railway communities—efficient, hygienic, anonymous—reflects the character of the new power of absentee capitalism in joint-stock organization, but the individualism of small-scale enterprise was stimulated through the growth of horse-drawn traffic to serve the railway centres. The railway labour force was large, but it was only a fraction of the 750,000 who were classified in 1881 as 'labour engaged in conveyance', almost as many as those occupied in the building trades and third after agriculture. The railways killed the coaching industry but they stimulated the passenger- and goods-carrying traffic by increasing the speed of deliveries and above all by increasing the size of towns. Urban workers needed more and more transport as their numbers grew; George Shillibeer brought the London omnibus from Paris in 1829; horse-drawn street trams came from America in the 1850s and spread steadily; they brought with them the granite sets because these were best for holding the rails; and the infinite variety of horse-drawn vehicles, above all the cab, the fly, and the omnibus spread the macadamized roads which had the advantage of saving the horses' feet.

With the spread of railways abroad the characteristic marks of the British railway industry began to be found in many unlikely places. British navvies were at work in France and Belgium from 1840. Morton Peto took his army of navvies into most of the countries of Europe and into much of America; the first standard gauge railway opened in Peru in 1851 was partly the work of British engineers; Thomas Brassey was building railways and docks in the Argentine in the 1860s and was said at one time to have had railways or docks under construction in four continents. The mileage of British railways grew from 4,600 in 1848 to 16,708 in 1886. World mileage rose from 4,000 in 1840 to 200,000 in 1880, and £163 m. of railway iron for this gigantic network was the product of British foundries. British iron had wellnigh girdled the earth in forty years, and on the way had touched into new life great areas of virgin soil which contributed by their production of food and raw material to stock the workshop and the larder of Britain as well as to raise the money wages of British workers. In its passage it had also generated incomes without providing the goods on which they could immediately be spent, and so paved the way for an expansion of the consumer goods industries when the long railway boom reached its inevitable end.

The repeal of the navigation acts in 1849 brought to an end 400 years of state protection of British shipping. In view of the advantages possessed by the U.S.A. in the supply of timber, and the skill of her ship-wrights, there were those who thought that it marked also the end of the British supremacy at sea; yet within thirty years, one-third of the world's shipping tonnage was British owned and a still larger proportion was British built. This astonishing transformation was mainly due to British leadership in metallurgy and marine engineering which began to give British shipping a margin of cheapness and quality during the later years of wood and sail, and overwhelmed all competition in the age of iron and steel. The American Civil War also contributed to British shipping supremacy by keeping America out of the market at a crucial stage of technical development, and after the war was over America directed her effort towards the conquest of the West rather than of the sea. In no department of the world's economic life was Britain's supremacy so complete and so long maintained.

Until the late 1830s Britain's progress in shipping had been slow. Free Traders attributed this to the numbing effects of protection and pointed to the fact that British shipping activities had grown twice as fast on 'unprotected routes' opened under the reciprocity agreements of 1824 as on the protected routes. It was also complained that British ship-builders preferred the rule-of-thumb approximations of the apprenticed ship-wrights to the mathematical niceties of the trained marine engineers. Depending on a thin stream from the engineering schools of the Royal Dockyards (trained with the aid of foreign textbooks since none existed in English) and on the guidance of the great engineering firms of Maudslay, Napier, the Rennies, Fairbairn, Scott-Russell, the more enterprising firms successfully took up the challenge of the American ship-wrights in the period of transition from wood and sail to iron and steam. From the launching of a new line of fast sailing clippers in 1837 on the Indian and Australian hauls, a new era of British ship-building began; and when, in 1851, the composite ships consisting of planks on iron frames were laid down, the leadership began to pass into British hands. Sailing ships entirely of iron began to compete successfully on the Australian and Far Eastern run in the 1850s; in the same decade, William Inman opened a line of screw-driven iron steamers between Liverpool and New York; Cunard began to build iron screw steamers for the Atlantic trade in 1862, and iron screw colliers began to ply between the N.E. coast and the Thames. Compound engines were introduced in the same year and by 1872 had reduced the consumption of coal by half. In 1869 the Suez Canal was opened and offered the nearer Orient to steam, but not to sail. Between 1865 and 1885 British steamship tonnage rose from one million to four; sailing tonnage fell from five million to three and a half. 'Single handed', says Sir John Clapham, 'Britain had created modern ship building.'

A factor in the transformation of the shipping industry, as of the steel industry, was the advance of precise engineering under the leadership of Joseph Whitworth and William Armstrong. Every marine engine and locomotive in the country, it was said, had the same screw thread for every given diameter, and the Whitworth machine shops at Manchester which produced the dies were supplying the world with machine parts made to gauge and perfectly interchangeable. William Armstrong, a lawyer by profession, patented a hydraulic crane in 1847 and went on to invent hydraulic machinery of every kind: grain elevators, pit-winding engines, lifts, capstans, swing- and draw-bridges, lock-gates, the mechanization for gun turrets. Hydraulic machinery was now coming into use in the average metal shop for flanging and riveting, for multiple punching and drilling. The mechanics of standardization were beginning to penetrate old industries which had hitherto withstood the impact of the machine; the manufacture of shoes and ready-made clothing was made possible by the application of power to the American sewing machine, and by 1871 the factory inspectors noted the existence of fifty-eight tailoring and clothing factories and 145 boot and shoe factories. The finishing had still to be done by armies of out-workers whose livelihood was made more rather than less secure (as in the hosiery industry) through the expansion of the market which the mechanization of the initial—and most laborious—processes made possible. The self-acting machinery from America also helped to mechanize the metallurgical industries of Birmingham; the manufacture of small arms, locks, brass tubes and electro-plating, metal bedsteads, cheap jewellery, steel pens, became partly or wholly factory industries, but the notorious trade of nail making was only crippled, not killed, by the machine-cut nails, owing to the preference of boot and shoe manufacturers for the hand-made nail for boot soles. Saw-grinding and file cutting machinery in the late 1850s, and later mechanical hammers for blade forging, all from America, were steps in the mechanization of the ancient cutlery trades.

From the 1860s the combination of standardization and scientific technology was preparing to make an impact on the pattern of living which presages the modern age, and among the achievements of these years are the bicycle, patented in 1868; and its mass production by 1880; the discoveries of William Perkins between 1856 and 1869 of the chemical potentialities of coal by-products for the dyeing industry; the invention of the electric light by Faraday in 1850 and the 'dynamo machine' in 1867; the opening of the trans-atlantic telegraph in 1866 and of the first telephone exchanges in London in 1879. Electric power was being used in the U.S.A. and on the Continent, but Britain, where coal was king, was slow to enter the electrical age. Experiments in refrigeration, going back to the successful production of laboratory ice at Edinburgh in 1810, resulted in the invention of Reece's freezing machine in 1867 which by 1880 could make fifteen tons of clear block ice a day from a ton and a half of coal; in February 1880 a cargo of frozen meat from Australia was landed at the London docks and the British tin plate industry, using Siemens's steel and a new process for spreading tin, was providing the material for the canning industries of Australia and America.

The flood of preserved meat and fruit which broke on the British market in the 1880s added to the tribulations of British farmers and helped to justify the title of 'The Great Depression' by which this period is known. On the industrial side, it had started in 1873, but with very different effects. The ending of the world railway boom in that year opened a new phase in the history of the British economy. There was a temporary cessation in foreign lending; a sharp fall in profits and prices and 'a widespread feeling of depression among the producing classes'. In spite of heavy investment, the rate of growth of the older industries began to fall while in the new industries of electricity and chemicals a decisive lead was built up by Germany and the U.S.A. Had there been an over-export of capital in the boom years that would have been better employed in modernizing home industries? Professor Cairncross[1] has argued, on the contrary, that capital exports served the nation well by expanding markets abroad, by providing cheap food, and by creating an income from overseas—an income that enabled Britain to meet the growing negative balance of payments arising largely through the increasing imports of cheap food in the last quarter of the century. The British economy continued to advance, though more slowly; and the decisive factor in its progress was the revolutionary effect of railways and shipping services which British enterprise had pioneered throughout the world. The great

[1] A. K. Cairncross, *Home and Foreign Investment*, Ch. IX.

fall in food prices was made possible more by a fall in freights than by sacrifices on the part of the primary producing countries;[1] and the stimulus that the railway and steamship age imparted to the economy generated new incomes for further investment not only in Britain but throughout the international trading area with which she had dealings. The take-off had become an unmistakable fact of British history, and a force of revolutionary significance for the entire world.

[1] See A. E. Musson, 'The Great Depression in Britain 1873–1896: A Reappraisal', *The Journal of Economic History*, xix, June 1959, and below, p. 82.

3

Agriculture and the Corn Laws

OF ALL THE INDUSTRIES subjected to these currents of technical and economic change, none was so kind to its innovators as agriculture. The major part of their capital consisted of the land itself, some of the best agricultural land in the world, with one of the best of agricultural climates; and under the stimulus of the English system of quasi-co-operative enterprise between landlord and tenant,[1] no land was more responsive to intelligent management and technical ingenuity. A typical example of the farmer's method was the work of James Small who discovered the optimum curve of the mould board of the plough by allowing the turning furrow to scour a soft wooden mould board to the position of minimum friction and so to settle the lines of the plough-breast down to our own, and presumably for all, time. The plough now became a product of precise engineering, and the firm of Ransome's of Norwich were able to marry the iron of Coalbrookdale to the empirical formula of the ploughman and produce for the world a scientifically designed tool of cultivation. Other, perhaps more important, innovations flowed from the same school of patient empiricism. The four-course rotation and the management of periodical leys provided winter keep which enabled graziers to effect a revolution in selective breeding and establish the pedigree stock industry which peopled the pastures of the world with British pedigree Shorthorns, Ayrshires, Herefords. Their success in sheep was no less remarkable. They were building on the lore of generations of English shepherds to whom a modern student of scientific

[1] See above, pp. 9-10.

breeding, Dr. Allen Fraser, pays a striking tribute: 'How did men who knew nothing of genetic science, of nutritional science, of veterinary science, with pastures unimproved, roots non-existent and cake undreamt of, produce breeds that have stamped an English seal on the faces of sheep of three continents?'[1] On this basis, Bakewell and Ellman, Colling, Coke and others in the eighteenth and nineteenth centuries built up the supremacy of British breeds, and the British workshop can claim pride of place in providing the sheep and cattle that helped to clothe and feed the growing millions all over the world.

These innovations had already performed a vital service in the land of their origin. They took place in an age when, in the vivid metaphor of Sir John Clapham, 'the swift growth of population was driving Ricardo's margin of cultivation visibly across the heaths and up the hills'. During the wars with France, the retreat of the margin of cultivation became a flight before the very real threat of famine, and some of the $1\frac{1}{4}$ million acres enclosed by parliamentary enactment between 1793 and 1815 tumbled down to grass in the post-war depression. The price of wheat fell from an average of 96s. a quarter for the last seven years of war to an average of 72s. for the first seven years of peace, but the continuous expansion of the home market under the pressure of 200,000 more mouths to feed every year provided opportunities to which most farmers and landlords were not slow to respond. The stimulus now was not high prices but low prices, and the reward went to the farmer who could make up for falling profits by increasing his turnover. Enclosure went ahead, especially on light soils. Areas of waste in Lincoln, Suffolk, Wiltshire, Devon were said, by an enthusiastic German visitor in the 1820s, to have been transformed as if by magic into cornfields, and Cobbett noted about the same time that 'those very ugly things, common fields, which have all the nakedness without the smoothness of the Downs' were gradually disappearing even from the uplands of Oxford and Cambridge, and by 1830 these two counties were nearly in line with the rest of England. The age-long battle with the fens was entering its last phase as a result of the application of the steam engine to scoop wheels to keep the water at a safe level; between Peterborough and Boston the fields were as flat as the table on which Cobbett wrote

[1] See R. Trow-Smith, *English Husbandry*, Chs. 8 and 9.

his *Rural Rides*, and sheep 'as fat as hogs' lay in the rich grass with which they were clothed. British agriculture was now equipped to adjust the methods of cultivation to the most productive use of the different kinds of soil and at the same time to increase the supply of natural and artificial fertilizer for the maintenance of output.

In farming language, it was now possible to fill 'the hungry gap'—the period of shortage between last year's hay and the new spring grass—which had been the farmer's nightmare from time immemorial. Not only turnips, but swedes—a hardy variety of turnip which could weather the early frosts—Dutch clover, rye-grass, rape, cabbages, enabled the pastoral farmer to stall-feed fatstock through the winter and the grain farmer to combine animal husbandry, especially for sheep, with arable farming. The upshot of this fundamental change in farming practice was that light soils which had lain in semi-idleness in common or waste were now brought into production and, after enclosure, were made to yield grain, meat, dairy products at a cost which threatened the traditional precedence of the heavy clay soils. To the farmer of the Midland clays, enclosure was a two-edged weapon: it might enable him to put his heavy arable down to grass or periodical leys and bring his lighter commons into four-course husbandry: but if, as might well happen on cold, wet land which would not carry turnips this choice was not open to him, he might find himself saddled with the expense and trouble of enclosure without being able to make up his losses through improved land use: Many enclosed parishes continued to farm with bare fallows and medieval rotation because the land permitted nothing else, but when the prop of wartime prices ceased to support this travesty of farming, landlords and farmers had to apply themselves afresh to the problem of heavy soil husbandry. They solved it through the development of scientific stock farming on permanent pastures and by mastering the art of deep drainage. They were assisted by the work of John Lawes who, in 1842, started both the manufacture of mineral superphosphates at Deptford and the researches which led to the establishment of the famous experimental station at Rothamsted, and of John Scragg, whose machine for the mass production of perforated drain pipes invented in the same year marked the final mastery of the technique of large-scale drainage.

One form of economy the farmers had scarcely begun to make on an appreciable scale, an economy in the use of labour. So far, this had not been an urgent necessity except in northern counties where the growth of large-scale industry provided an alternative livelihood to agricultural labour. In Lancashire, where labour was scarce, the threshing machine spread from the great modern farms on the Scottish lowlands in the last decade of the eighteenth century, but its progress south was slow. In 1824 it was said actually to be in retreat in Huntingdon as there was plenty of pauperized labour to do the work; and the stricter administration of the Poor Law after 1834 increased rather than diminished the supply of labour and reduced the incentive to replace the machines destroyed in the Labourers' Revolt of 1830. The only labour-saving device in widespread use was the hay tedder, which was popular on the dairy farms round London and does not seem to have met with the disapproval of Captain Swing (the mysterious leader of the rural machine wreckers of 1830). Even in the 1840s there were areas in the south which remained immune from the mechanical urge; in Surrey the winnowing machine was still unknown and within a couple of miles of Brighton it was possible to see six bullocks drawing an all-wooden plough—'linking the days of Queen Victoria to those of the Empress Matilda'. But the repeal of the Corn Laws shook the most conservative of farmers into new ways of thinking, and except where labour was still inhibited from movement by the fear of removal under the Settlement Laws, the substitution of scythe and sickle and hand-winnowing by mechanical reaping and winnowing was only a matter of time. The Scottish farmers were already in the field with experimental reaping machines, and by 1852 the problem was solved. By mid-century, the age of scientific farming had dawned; the railway was bringing the farmers into a new relationship with the great urban markets, and British agriculture was turning with profound but, as yet, needless misgivings to face the challenge of free trade.

To think of agriculture as a single industry, however, is misleading. It is a group of industries with different problems and sometimes with divergent interests. Together they employed in 1831 nearly a million families, more than four and a half million persons, or 28 per cent of the nation. Ten years later, when industry and trade had grown far faster than agriculture, it still contributed more than a third of the national income and considerably more than all the branches of manufacturing industries together. In spite of the act of 1832, members of the landed interest monopolized the offices of State, and on the eve of the decision on the Corn Laws, the farmers could still be described by Charles Villiers, the free trade leader, as 'the people who *really* have the government of the country in their hands'.

They were engaged in three main branches of production: grain farming providing raw materials for milling, brewing, baking, distilling, starch-making; sheep farming for wool and mutton; dairy and fatstock farming, providing not only meat and dairy produce but raw materials for the manufacture of tallow, soap, vegetable oil, glue, and leather. The cultivated acreage—27 million acres according to an estimate of 1851—was almost equally divided between arable and permanent pasture, the midland and western counties being two-thirds in grass, the eastern counties being two-thirds in arable.

The great majority of farmers were engaged in at least two, and frequently in all, these branches of the industry, especially since the introduction of roots and clover into the rotation made it possible to pursue mixed farming on soils that had hitherto been considered too light for successful arable cultivation; but there were specialists who concentrated on one or other of the main branches, and the division between those engaged primarily in animal husbandry and those in grain farming was one of interest as well as of outlook. Graziers of Leicestershire and dairy farmers of Lancashire wanted cheap feeding stuffs and a prosperous urban market of which they enjoyed a monopoly. Wool farmers alone were without natural or legislative protection, the duty on wool having been virtually abolished in 1825, but most of the home clip and of the growing import of fine wools from Australia was absorbed by the home market and the surplus found its way abroad, especially to France. Since most farmers depended to some extent on the domestic corn market, they gave support to the policy of maintaining corn prices through protection; but neither farming interest nor farming opinion were all on one side; many landlords were as much interested in the returns from coal mines, railways, and urban properties as in the price of corn, and if the agricultural labourers sometimes quenched the oratory of Anti-Corn Law speakers in the water of the village duck-pond, they also burned ricks in support of the cause and are reported to have sometimes met Anti-Corn Law emissaries armed with pitchforks and asking if the day of deliverance had dawned.

The case for agricultural protection rested exclusively on the difficulties of the producers of corn. They were at the centre of the controversy and tended to speak for the entire industry. Unlike the fat stock and dairy farmers they had not only to face foreign competition but the more intractable consequences of an expanding but inelastic demand. A fall in the price of meat would be partially cushioned by an increase in the amount consumed; the relatively fixed demand for bread corn caused prices to fluctuate disproportionately to the changes in the size of the harvest; and since it had been a patriotic duty during the war to produce grain at any cost, there were many farmers whose survival depended upon the maintenance of near wartime prices to meet higher wages, rents, taxes, poor rates and interest rates, and the unchanging tithe of the produce, whatever the price, demanded by the Church. Moreover, the products of animal husbandry could command not only more steady but relatively higher prices: an inquiry in 1851 showed that whereas butter and wool had doubled in price since 1770, and meat was higher by 70 per cent, the price of wheat was the same, and rents for both types of land had roughly doubled.

Small farmers shared, along with large farmers, in the prosperity of the war years and they may actually have risen in number, but they appear to have been the chief sufferers from the post-war prices, which fell faster than overhead costs, especially poor rates. The reduction in their numbers, however, was by no means catastrophic, and in 1831 nearly half the total number of farming units still consisted of small family farms, i.e. those of farmers who employed no labour other than that of their families. They numbered 130,500 compared with 144,600 who employed outside labour, and were found in every county and sometimes, as in the Lincolnshire fens, and on the hills of Cumberland and Westmorland and west Wales, they were on a continental peasant scale. Enclosure had reduced the numbers of small farmers by obliterating commons and so cutting away the lowest rung of the rural ladder by which they ascended from the landless; it also assisted the process of consolidation by putting heavy charges on small freeholders and enabling landlords to reorganize their tenancies on a larger basis, but it did not, as a well-known school book still confidently tells us, cause the small farmer 'to disappear from the land'. In the case of west Wales, it led to an alarming increase of small farmers and a dangerous pressure of population.[1]

In social terms, the change was far more drastic. The large farmers were usually larger and richer than before the war and they shared with their landlords the heightened social pretensions which wartime prosperity had encouraged. A new ruthlessness entered into the administration of the unspeakable Game Laws.[2] The gulf between the rural social classes had widened both in fact and in feeling, especially in the southern and eastern counties where the growth of population provided a surplus over the needs of agriculture and the decaying rural industries. Allowances in aid of wages were to be found in northern as well as southern parishes, but it was only in the south and east where large-scale industry offered no alternative livelihood that they formed part of the regular wage structure, and large farmers had their labour bill partially met for them by the parish. Small farmers and even scrap holders had to pay poor rates without enjoying the advantage of subsidized labour, but were not allowed to draw poor relief themselves until they were landless. The Poor Law Amendment Act of 1834 tried to put an end to the allowance system, but the essential problem of an over-populated countryside, with labourers crowded in squalid 'open' villages and walking out to work in 'closed' villages two or three miles away, remained essentially untouched until steam transport by land and sea effected a more rational distribution of the national labour force.

The growth of the non-agricultural population provided a continuously expanding market for the products of British farms, which, by their increased production, almost kept pace with the demand. In the first decade of the century, the number of persons in Great Britain fed on foreign wheat was between 600,000 and 800,000 out of a total population of nearly 12 million; in the fourth decade the number was between 900,000 and 1,200,000 out of a total of $17\frac{1}{2}$ million. Britain was still largely self-supporting in wheat and virtually so in animal products. This increased production was accomplished by a labour force that continued to grow

[1] See David Williams, *The Rebecca Riots: A Study in Agrarian Discontent* (1955).
[2] See especially J. L. and Barbara Hammond, *The Village Labourer*, Ch. VII.

only very slowly between the 1820s and 1850s; and since, during the period, there were few labour-saving innovations, increased production must therefore be attributed to the employment of capital in improving the soil, in draining, manuring, and above all in taking in new land suitable for mixed farming.

In spite of these favourable circumstances there were periods of farmers' distress in 1820–3, 1826–9, and 1832–6 when good harvests brought prices down below remunerative levels for the weaker farmers, and there were cries for government help. Other causes of complaint were the deflationary monetary policy of the government exemplified in the return to gold and the reduction of the small-note issue; the weight of taxes and above all poor rates which fell more slowly than prices; the instability of the country banks, of which over a dozen collapsed, on the average, every year between 1815 and 1830, and never a year with less than three; tithes which took their quota in good years and bad and represented a tax of 10 per cent on the produce of every fresh acre that was brought into cultivation by the labour and capital of the farmer; the burden of statute labour on roads which served the traffic of the nation rather than that of the parish. Some of these grievances could be met; poor rates and tithes were dealt with in the Acts of 1834 and 1836; statute labour was abolished by the Act of 1835 and financial stability grew with the steady strengthening of the banking system after the Act of 1826. But one problem could be solved only by the farmers and landlords themselves, the problem of the cold clay soils in need of drainage. Soils of this kind—in the Weald, Shropshire, Worcester, Somerset, the Vale of Gloucester—yielded 12–16 bushels per acre against a national average of 20–22, and a maximum yield of the light friable soils of Norfolk of 30. As many as six ploughings and five harrowings were necessary, it was said, to produce a seed bed, and on some clay farms it was impossible to grow turnips at all. Rents on these farms frequently fell to pre-war levels and large areas gradually and rightly were laid down to grass. With the development of the four-course rotation, the advantage lay with light soil mixed farming, and between 1802 and 1844 no less than half a million acres were enclosed of which 60 per cent was taken from the uncultivated waste. The new mixed farms on the light soils and the old grazing and dairying areas of Leicestershire, Northants., and the West Country scarcely felt the effects of the price fall; and even in the heavy arable areas where drainage was proceeding there was little complaint. It was mainly to meet the difficulties of the clay farmers who relied on the grain crop to meet their fixed overhead charges that protection found its justification.

The Corn Law of 1815 which forbade the taking of imported wheat from bond until the home price reached 80s. a quarter proved too rigid, and the sliding scale of 1828, which was intended to adjust the degree of protection to the fall in price, took its place. Farmers still complained on the grounds that it encouraged merchants to hold up supplies until the prices reached 72s. a quarter, with the consequence of an influx of imported corn at a nominal duty fixed by the scale, followed by a speedy fall of price; and the British farmer who came late to the market might find that he had missed the tide at the flood. The merchant, on the other hand, complained that a slight fall, e.g. from 73s. to 69s. raised the duty from 1s. to 13s. 8d. which made importation a ruinously speculative business. It also discouraged the foreign producer from providing a steady supply and encouraged speculative buying in anticipation of a run of bad harvests. The general effect was to keep prices higher than they would otherwise have been, especially in years of moderate crops when, owing to the relatively high duties, there were practically no imports at all. In these years, reserve supplies were called upon with the result that, if the following harvest was deficient, there were no reserves available and prices rose to very high levels before the rise could be checked by imported supplies. That was notably the cause of the food crisis of 1838–9, when the price rose to 70s. a quarter and importation reached a record figure of 2,590,000 quarters. In 1841 this record was broken, and again in 1842 when the imports reached 2,977,000 quarters owing to the expectation of importers that the condition of shortage would continue. The harvest, however, was exceptionally good; the price fell and the corn had to be entered at a price and a duty that carried a loss to the importers. Thus the outflow of gold for foreign corn was greater than it need have been had there been no inducement to gamble on the continuance of high prices, and the loss to home producers from the switch from industrial products to meeting the basic need of food supply, especially bread, was a regular feature of these years of high prices. Years of farmers' prosperity under protection tended to coincide with workers' distress owing to the combined effects of high prices and unemployment.

The protection of agriculture was felt to be a form of privilege. It provided the ground work for the hostility that grew up against the landlords as a class and provided confirmation of the economists' argument that through their monopoly of the soil, the landlords were the natural enemies of the entire community. Classical theory taught that wages were kept down to subsistence level owing to the pressure of population and the limitation of the wage fund; profits had a tendency to fall owing to the competition of capital; only rents would rise with the taking in of new land for the support of the increasing population. Profits and wages which were the fruits of abstinence and toil would be sacrificed to 'rent-eaters' who neither laboured nor put by; Joseph Chamberlain's jibe, 'They toil not neither do they spin', was anticipated in spirit if not in form by half a century, and economists had the unusual experience of having their theories echoed by poets and pamphleteers.

Did the landlords deserve this stream of obloquy? It was the price they had to pay for the enormous privileges they enjoyed as virtual monopolists of the soil. The system of entail under which estates were generally held aimed at ensuring that they should pass intact in the same family from generation to generation. As the New Domesday Book was to show in 1874, half the country was owned by less than 8,000 persons, a concentration of ownership that had been frenziedly denounced by Chartists and Free Traders, but which was not incompatible with perhaps the most successful phase in the history of English landlordism. What was the economic role of the landlord? Ideally, it was to exercise a stewardship of the national patrimony in the fertility of the soil, which landlords claimed as their private property; they should do this by encouraging good husbandry through a wise and beneficent oversight of their tenants so that yields should rise and fertility remain unimpaired. Under these conditions the rent was no more than a return upon investment in a concern in which the landlord took a share of the risks as well as of the profits along with the tenant. James Caird showed that a number of landlords fulfilled this ideal: the Duke of Wellington, Earl Spencer, Lord Yarborough, the Duke of Portland, Mr. Philip Pusey, Sir Robert Peel, and numerous others. Some of the best were retired manufacturers

C

who gave to their land the same kind of direction that had gained them success in business. They spent with a free hand on drainage, good buildings, and new fertilizers, charging a moderate interest on the outlay and giving security to the tenant through long leases or by establishing confidence in other ways. The confidence of tenants in landlords such as these encouraged them to invest their own capital in improvements even without the guarantee of security or compensation for unexhausted improvements, and an informal arrangement based on mutual confidence was often found to work better than legal instruments enforceable in the courts. At its best, the British landlord system was well calculated—perhaps better than any other—to promote good husbandry through the tacit co-operation of landlord and tenant in pursuit of an objective in which they had a common interest. But the number of landlords who could be said to fulfil the role was not large. In the post-war years, many landlords would not or could not carry out improvements; some were encumbered with inherited debts under the system of entail; others were ignorant and careless and appointed stewards as ignorant and careless as themselves; on all but the best estates farm buildings were deplorable, offering little protection to shivering cattle and in some cases a peril to man and beast in every high wind; on too many estates the interests of agriculture were sacrificed to those of sport, and the owners of such estates earned the contempt of an industrious age as a class of parasites living on the labour of others.

The system, however, remained intact and no satisfactory substitute has yet been found. This is largely due to the success with which, in spite of its weaknesses, it met the challenge of the time. There was a steady taking-in of new land until the middle of the century, and the adjustment to light soil mixed husbandry was gradually accomplished; drainage advanced partly by the use of the mole plough and also as a result of a new process in the 1840s for the mass production of perforated pipes which raised maximum daily production per machine from 1,000 to 20,000 feet. Two large loans, initiated by Sir Robert Peel and renewed by his successor, provided cheap capital, and the energy—sometimes misdirected—with which deep drainage was undertaken rapidly removed the greatest single obstacle to improved farming for corn. The work of the Royal Agricultural Society in spreading the knowledge of new

fertilizers and the experiments of John Lawes at his farm at Rothamsted began to bear fruit, and a few farmers' sons were to be found
among the sons of lawyers, clergymen, and army officers at the first
agricultural college at Cirencester. Among the two thousand imple-
ments exhibited at the Royal Show in 1850 were reapers, mowing
machines, horse rakes, hay tedders, and other labour-saving devices.
The steam thresher which had made such an inauspicious début
in 1830 was now in general use; steam ploughing was spreading
from Scotland and steam transport was widening the urban market
and extending specialization deeper into the countryside. Whatever
may be said of the British landlord system, it was instrumental in
these years in bringing about a transformation of British agricultural methods.

Whether the farmers had ever needed protection from foreign
imports is a debatable question; by 1846, one of their own number,
Sir Robert Peel, had satisfied himself that they needed it no longer.
The extraordinary success of his reforms of the tariff converted him
to the logic of free trade, and he applied it to agriculture to the dis-
may of the majority of his party who wanted free trade for every-
body but themselves. If their leader could have foreseen the effects
on British agriculture of the coming revolution in world transport
he would almost certainly have agreed with them; but this was
delayed for a quarter of a century during which British farmers and
landlords effected immense improvements and enjoyed unprecedented prosperity. Between 1850 and 1870 the improvement of the
best farmers became the practice of the average—'a general up-
heaval of the middling and the worst'. Machine threshing became
general and machine mowing gradually superseded the scythe.
Above all, the progress in drainage went forward under the influence
of the loans of 1846 and 1850 with new vigour, and it continued
under inspection by Enclosure Commissioners after the Treasury
grants were exhausted. On the strong lands of Huntingdon, drainage was said to have doubled production in the twenty years before
1868; it 'had worked wonders' in the clay lands of Sheppey and the
same could be said of most clay districts. About £12 m. had been
advanced between 1846 and 1876 of which £9 m. probably went in
drainage. Chemical manures, especially superphosphate of lime,
were becoming more widely used by discerning farmers. Rotations
were becoming more elastic and better suited to the wide variety of

British soils; the spread of the railway network enabled grain farmers to diversify production by supplying distant urban markets with livestock and dairy products, and dairy-farming itself was beginning to respond to the growth of knowledge of scientific feeding for milk production. The close connexion between arable and pasture farming enabled British farming to carry a bigger head of livestock in proportion to its area than any part of Europe, and there were as many sheep in the United Kingdom, it was said by a French visitor in 1851-2, as in the whole of France and in far better condition. 'In no country at any time has the combination of arable farming and sheep farming been so successfully carried out as in nineteenth-century Britain.'[1] In terms of income tax returns, farming incomes rose in England and Wales by 21 per cent, in Scotland by 41 per cent between 1850 and 1878, and the rise was most pronounced in the pastoral areas and most rapid in the second half of the period.

For grain farmers the end of the honeymoon came with the bad harvests of 1873 and 1875 and especially 1879. It would have come earlier but for the wars on the Continent and the U.S.A. which gave British farmers a fortuitous respite from some of the effects of free trade. The cessation of the wars and the advance of transport brought the British grain farmers face to face with the harsh realities of free trade; the time had come when a bad harvest no longer brought consolation in a disproportionate rise of prices. Foreign imports kept down the price and a lower yield was punished by a lower return. Five bad harvests between 1852 and 1862 had yielded on an average 24 bushels to the acre and an average price of 62s. 1d. per quarter; the five bad years of the seventies yielded 19 bushels per acre at an average price of 49s. 10d. The import of wheat which had been 48 per cent of the whole consumption in 1868-78 rose to between 60 and 70 per cent. 'There can be no doubt', Porter had written in 1851, 'that for a much longer period than twenty years, the soil of these islands will continue to yield the largest proportion of the food of the inhabitants.' British shipping and American railways had shortened the period of grace for the British grain farmer, and he had no choice but to accept the implications of the free trade argument.

This was made easier for him than might appear by the relative

[1] See Clapham, op. cit., vol. ii, pp. 274-5.

immunity of meat and dairy farming to which many farmers could turn, at least in part, especially after the completion of the railway network. The import of beef was only 9 per cent of consumption and of mutton 7 per cent. There was increasing competition in dairy produce but prices and consumption of British products both in the aggregate and per head remained steady. Only wool farmers could match the complaints of the grain farmers; wool prices fell by nearly a half and the corn and wool farms of the Lincolnshire wolds faced ruin. Elsewhere, the clay lands of the Midlands and the mainly grain lands of East Anglia were having recourse to rent abatements and remissions in accordance with traditional British practice; for England and Wales as a whole, the reduction was 22·6 per cent between 1878-9 and 1893-4; for Scotland, which grew less wheat, it was 18·5 per cent; for the counties affected it was far more; about a million and a half acres were added to the permanent pasture, and the balance which had been held so evenly between arable and pastoral farming was decisively changed. Difficult adjustments were again being asked of the arable farmer; the drafts on his adaptability which free trade required were at last being presented, and Scottish farmers sometimes showed they could meet them where English farmers had failed; but the nation as a whole cheerfully accepted the implication which Porter had drawn a generation earlier:

The limited extent of cultivable land necessarily limits the number of labourers employed upon it; the additional hands will consequently have to betake themselves to the manufacture of articles desired in other countries and those hands will be as effectually engaged in producing food, when employed in the cotton mills of Lancashire, and the iron mines of Yorkshire and Staffordshire, as if their industry were applied directly to the cultivation of the soil.

4
Foreign Trade and Fiscal Policy

IN THE PERIOD of transition to industrialism the growth of foreign trade assumed a new importance in the development not only of the economy of Britain, but also of the economies of the widening range of countries that traded with her. The chief new influence that it exerted sprang from the development of the cotton industry which enjoyed the double advantage of revolutionary innovation both in the manufacture of the finished article at home and in the production of the raw material abroad. The rapid conquest of new markets which was thus made possible enabled the industry to take advantage of economies of scale which the home market alone could never have justified and the increasing demand for new cotton and dye-stuffs created a growing market for the export of British goods and services. The U.S.A. and Spanish America were the two areas most affected by this development of textiles; but after 1830, a third area, Australasia, was summoned into existence owing to the unprecedented demands of the woollen industry which were far beyond the capacity of the older countries of origin, Spain and Germany, to supply. The innovations in other branches of industry influenced the pattern of trade by reducing British dependence on overseas supplies of iron and by opening a steadily widening avenue for exports of the products of iron, pottery, glass, and machinery industries.

The application of machinery to production also had the effect of causing a more rapid fall of price of exported manufactures than of imported primary produce and, from 1816, exports were never sufficient to pay for imports. The adverse balance was met by the earnings of British shipping and the services of British commercial and financial agencies. Not only was the balance met, but a surplus was available for investment abroad. This outflow of savings, mounting from a total of perhaps £10 m. in 1815 to nearly £100 m. in 1825 and £700 m. in 1870, financed the economic expansion of borrowing countries at a time when their own incomes were rising too slowly to provide a surplus for large-scale investment. Thus the process of industrialization was stimulated both at home and abroad through the mechanism of British trade; and since the industrial sector gave the highest rate of return and encouraged the most rapid rate of capital accumulation, the role of foreign trade was a factor in economic growth not only in Britain but in all parts of the world which had dealings with her.

The technical advantages enjoyed by British industry in the last quarter of the eighteenth century were quickly reflected in the figures of foreign trade. The gap which had been opened between Britain and her competitors was widened during the years of war, and the flood of British exports which had to meet when it was over was met by a sharp raising of tariffs both in Europe and America. In 1815 exports reached a peak figure of £51 m., but tariffs rose and prices fell, and for the four years 1819-22 the value was down to an average of £36·3 m., a fall of nearly 30 per cent, though in volume the fall was less than 1 per cent. At the same time the growth of population, the return of the armed forces to civilian life, and the influx of Irish immigrants created a labour surplus which was reflected in manifestations of social distress familiar to all students of the period.

The expansion of foreign trade was, therefore, vital to the stability of the nation; but the physical basis on which the structure of foreign trade rested was relatively slender. Of the £36 m. of exports in 1820, cotton goods accounted for £16½ m., or 47 per cent, and woollens and linens for 20 per cent, metals and glass for 10 per cent. There was also an illegal and therefore unrecorded export of machinery. After the war, the movement grew, and the Acts of 1824 and 1825 which removed the restriction on the emigration of workmen and permitted the export of machinery by licence, were a recognition of the fact that the British industrial revolution was becoming an international event. By 1830 total exports had crept up to £38·3 m., but in volume were nearly half as big again as in 1815; the proportion of cotton goods had risen to over half (£19·3 m.); other textiles accounted for £7 m., raw materials—coal, copper, lead, wool, china clay—and partially manufactured goods—pig-iron, bar-iron—made up £6·9 m.; hardware, cutlery, and a sus-piciously small item of £240,000 'for machinery and mill work' made up the rest. By 1835–40 (inc.) the average value of exports had moved up to nearly £50 m., a surprising advance in view of the many alarms of those years; cotton held its place with £24 m., a rise of 32 per cent in value but, owing to cost-reducing economies described elsewhere, a doubling in terms of volume; wool accounted for £6 m., leaving about £20 m. for everything else. 'It is not sur-prising', says Sir John Clapham, 'that Britain's foreign trade presented itself almost as a problem in cotton or that Manchester claimed a great share in the determination of the commercial policy of the country.'

The problem of commercial policy was greatly influenced by two decisions taken in the years of turmoil and falling prices at the end of the war: the first was the Corn Law of 1815 which, largely as a result of the attacks upon it by Ricardo, focused the attention of thinking men upon the relation of exports to imports and the influence which could be exercised upon the purchasing power of foreign customers by fiscal policy. The second was the vote passed in 1816 by a surprisingly narrow majority—of 238 to 201—and against the will of the government, to abolish income tax. As a result of the vote, the landed interest were relieved of £8 m. and other income tax payers of £6 m., a total of £14 m. out of a budget of £72 m. It was therefore necessary to continue all the war taxes, to impose new indirect taxation of £5 m., and to raise a loan.

The government strove to reduce the intolerable load of taxa-tion by economies of all kinds and by reducing the service on the debt, and by 1830 national expenditure was down to £51 m., made up of £36 m. by customs and excise and £2¼ m. by window tax and hearth duty, and by a variety of 'assessed taxes'—on carriages, armorial bearings, dogs, guns, man servants, and by legacy and stamp duties. Subsequent governments abolished the excise on leather, printed calicoes, and other articles in com-mon consumption between 1830 and 1834, but to ardent free

traders the shadow of indirect taxation and above all the taxation
of imported corn lay across the path of economic and social progress.

There are different views as to the weight which should be given
to these obstacles to the export trade. Sir John Clapham points to
the blank walls of bans and prohibition erected after the war by
France and Russia and to the increasing tendency of the German
Zollverein to tax British manufactured textiles. Conceivably, the
Corn Laws and British duties on German linens helped the rise of
Zollverein tariffs, but it was unlikely, he thinks, that a change of
policy would have opened 'a much better vent' for British textiles
in European markets. In any case, the rise in value of British exports
from £35,600,000 between 1825 and 1829 to £50 m. a decade later
would have been regarded as satisfactory in any age 'less conscious
of its industrial power'.

In his analysis of the exports for 1830, however, he gives a
number of examples of the relation between imports and exports
which suggest that the fiscal system was less innocuous than it is
made to appear. He notes that the markets with high purchasing
power were among the best customers. The U.S.A. took £6·1 m.
largely paid for by raw cotton; the West Indies took £2·8 m. paid
for by sugar enjoying preferential tariffs; S. America and Mexico
took £5·2 m. having been financed by British capital exports;
Scandinavia and Russia, however, took only £1·7 m. against £1·9 m.
of British North America. It was not 'natural', he says, that Scandinavia and Russia should be such poor customers; but 'the British
parliament had willed it' by putting a duty of 55s. a load (equivalent
to a ton) on European timber against 10s. on Canadian timber. The
consumption of coffee was abysmally low, but it doubled to 1¼ lb.
per annum per head when duty on West Indian coffee was reduced
from 1s. to 6d.; tea, which paid 100 per cent, was 'held tightly in
the grip of the East India Company', and remained at 1¼ or possibly
1½ lb. per head per annum all through the 1820s and, at 4s. to 8s.
per lb., was beyond the reach of the poorer labourers.

It may also be shown that the most substantial growth took place
in the markets of Asia, Latin America, and South Europe, whereas
North Europe showed no marked upward change. Mr. Matthews
in his *Study of the Trade Cycle* has argued that the most important
single factor governing exports to the former group of markets was
the availability of means of remitting payments, and the largest of

these, the Asiatic market, was assisted in its growth by the multi-lateral settlement of accounts based on the enormous import of raw cotton by Britain from the U.S.A. The favourable American balance against Britain which it created enabled America to meet her adverse balance with the Orient by means of bills on London and this provided a convenient means of remitting to Britain the earnings of her merchants in the Far East.

The fiscal system affected the home as well as the foreign market through the excise on goods in common use. Every yard of calico consumed at home paid $3\frac{1}{2}d.$, duties on glass were so heavy and vexatious that technical progress was stifled and home consumption actually declined between 1812 and 1829; but exports of glass, which paid no duty, rose. Soap which paid $1d.$ per lb. in 1800 paid $3d.$ in 1815 and paper paid duties ranging from 15 per cent to 200 per cent according to quality. Edward Baines said that when the various duties on cotton goods were removed in 1831 a cotton dress with good fast colours that formerly cost $4s.$ could be bought for $2s.$; Joseph Hume in 1850 said that if the duties on bricks and timber were removed a cottage which cost £60 could be built for £40. The excise on bricks went in that year; glass duties had already gone in 1845; soap was freed in 1853 and paper in 1861; but before this welcome relief could be given, a fiscal battle had been fought and won which ranks with the greatest events in British history.

The passing of the Corn Law of 1815, it has been said, opened the 'Great Debate' between protection and free trade. Petitions against it poured in from manufacturing centres; working men demonstrated against it in London and twenty-one members of the House of Lords showed that the landed interest were not entirely of one mind by voting against it. It signalized the beginning of the struggle between the landed interest and the commercial interest which opened the door to a working alliance between industrialists and working men; free trade could be presented as the answer to unemployment, and man and master could eventually be made to see their common interest in pursuit of it. The abstract assumptions on which the alliance was to be based were set forth in classic form in the petition to the House of Commons drawn up in 1820 by Thomas Tooke to which he obtained, not without difficulty, the signatures of 'a considerable number of the most wealthy and enterprising houses in London'. It was followed shortly afterwards by one from Manchester, and another from Glasgow; but commercial opinion was slow to catch fire. The process of conversion made better progress in government circles; the Chancellor of the Exchequer gave warning that foreign buyers were being deprived of the means to pay for British exports, and the Prime Minister, Lord Liverpool, let it be known that he knew his fiscal duty but was unable to perform it. The government knew its duty in other ways and did it. In pursuit of its policy of putting down the trade in slaves it undertook the suppression of the Barbary pirates in 1816 and made the high seas safe for international trade, especially for the trade of weaker states. In 1821 it implemented its declared policy of returning to cash payments and restored the pre-war gold basis of international exchange in the belief that free gold and trade expansion went hand in hand. Free trade was postponed for more than a generation, but the provision of a stable gold basis for the world's greatest trading nation was a factor of strength in a growing world economy. In 1822, the recognition of the new republics in Central and South America was accompanied by relaxation of the Navigation Laws by which the new countries were promoted to equality with the U.S.A. and were permitted to export to Britain in their own ships, and the countries of Europe were at the same time allowed to share in colonial trade in return for reciprocal concessions, but Britain kept the monopoly of the long hauls within the Empire. Other reforms included the removal of restrictions on the import and export of wool and the substitution of a 30 per cent duty on silk imports in place of total prohibition, and the sliding scale of duties on corn.

Fortunately, William Huskisson, President of the Board of Trade, who initiated the first inroad into the protective system, was favoured by high returns of the revenue from 1823 and by the effects of government economies, and he persuaded Parliament to make reductions of duties which cost the Exchequer more than £4 m. a year—a reduction of over 8 per cent on a budget of £55 m.; he legalized the emigration of skilled workmen and was only prevented from removing duties on the export of machinery by the lively protests of the manufacturers who remained protectionist at heart, and he had to accept instead a system of export by licence.

The manufacturers could also point to the slow progress of

British exports in spite of all their efforts to capture new markets. Between 1816 and 1830 there was an actual fall of 8 per cent (from £41·7 m. to £38·3 m.) although in volume there had been a rise of 64 per cent. Export prices were falling faster than import prices, and the terms of trade were turning sharply against Britain. It can be shown, however, that the cotton industry bore the main burden of this downward trend of export prices in terms of import prices: whereas the price of manufactured goods as a whole fell by more than 50 per cent the price of exports other than cotton goods fell by little more than 30 per cent; in fact rather less than import prices. By means of striking price economies the cotton industry could claim that it was holding the pass for the export trade and was making up in volume what was lost in value.

The partial closure of European markets to British imports of which merchants complained was mitigated by smuggling through Dutch and German ports whence the goods found their way via the great fairs of Frankfurt and Leipzig to eastern Europe. Germany provided the best British market in Europe but the proportion—though not the volume—of Manchester goods exported to European countries tended to decline, and they consisted to an increasing extent of twist and yarn rather than of manufactured goods. The formation of the *Zollverein* threatened to replace the inefficient fiscal system of the old German states with a solid wall of tariffs with an alarming tendency to rise against certain types of manufactured goods. Dr. John Bowring, an official of the Board of Trade who made a special study of the German market, convinced himself that the British Corn Laws must be held responsible for this, and that the admission of German corn was the only way of securing German tariff concessions; moreover this should be made quickly, before the supply of German corn was absorbed by the needs of the rising German population, and the bargaining power of the British market thereby reduced.

The relatively unprotected markets of the East were more responsive to the cost-reducing economies of Lancashire. By concentrating on cheap calicoes for Indian and Far Eastern markets, British exports to the East had risen from less than a million yards in 1814 to over fifty-seven million yards in 1832; there was also a growing export of finer products; the Dacca muslins which were considered to be of unapproachable beauty were being superseded by Manchester goods, and 'the shawls of Cashmere', it was said in 1832, 'are being pushed from the market and employ about 6,000 looms instead of 30,000 as in by-gone days'. A vexatious restriction to further advance lay nearer home in the monopoly of the China trade by the East India Company. In 1833 this trade was thrown open and the expansion of Asiatic trade provided a welcome but unspectacular stimulus to British exports. The American market oscillated violently under the influence of fluctuating domestic policies and the ebb and flow of British credits. In the boom of 1835–6 it absorbed nearly a quarter of the total of British exports but the average was nearer one-sixth and tended to contract rather than expand. The over-all picture as presented by Mr. Imlah[1] is as follows:

Export outlets for products of the United Kingdom

	1816–20	1832–6	1838–42	Per cent change from 1816–20 to 1838–42
	(in £ at current prices)			
North Europe	£11·4 m.	£9·8 m.	£12·8 m.	+ 12
South Europe	7·3	7·5	9·5	+ 30
Africa	0·4	1·1	1·7	+ 325
Asia	3·4	5·2	7·9	+ 132
U.S.A.	7·0	8·6	6·5	− 7
Brit. N. Amer. & W. Indies	7·0	5·1	5·8	− 31 [− 17?]
Foreign W. Indies	1·0	1·2	1·1	+ 10
Central & S. America	2·8	5·0	5·4	+ 93
	£40·3 m.	£43·7 m.	£50·5 m.	+ 25

The increase of British exports was confined to the four regions of new development—south Europe, Africa, Asia, and Central and South America, the established markets of north Europe, the U.S.A., and British North America were taking slightly less at the end of the period than at the beginning.

The growth of the cost of imports was faster than that of exports and the visible trade deficit grew from £9 m. in 1816–20 to £24 m. in 1836–40. British shipping services contributed substantially to

[1] A. H. Imlah, *The Economic Elements in the Pax Britannica* (1958), p. 129.

the closing of the gap but hardly in proportion to the opportunities created by the immense growth in the volume of trade. Between 1816–20 and 1838–42 the volume of imports rose by 109 per cent and of exports and re-exports by 119 per cent, but owing to the steep fall of freights, earnings rose by only 18 per cent. Shipping interests opposed every suggestion of relaxation of the ancient system of protection under the Navigation Laws but they themselves were victims of the system owing to the high prices they had to pay for timber. There is some reason, also, to think they were lacking in enterprise. By the late 1830s, some of the shipping lines were showing what could be done by better service and faster ships on the unprotected routes; and according to the evidence submitted by G. R. Porter of the Board of Trade in 1847, British tonnage on these routes had grown almost twice as fast as on the controlled empire routes.

Income from foreign investments, important though it was in balancing the national accounts, was precarious and fluctuating. Between 1818 and 1830 British capital to the amount of £42 m. was invested in the bonds of foreign governments but by 1831 nearly half were in default. By 1838 investments in the U.S.A. are estimated to have reached $174 m. (nearly one-quarter of the total) and almost the whole was in default in 1842 and some of it was repudiated. In these circumstances it is instructive to see how the balance of payments was met. Between 1816–20 and 1836–40, the visible adverse balance had risen from £8·9 m. to £23·9 m. and the net balance on current account had fallen from £7·22 m. to £2·62 m.; the profits on shipping and services were relatively stagnant until 1836 when, for the first time, they rose above the level of 1816–20; this improvement, together with the rise of income from interest and dividends, prevented the return from showing a negative net balance. In the years 1840 and 1842 a negative balance was shown, and Britain drew on her capital to the amount of £2·3 m. and £0·6 m. respectively.

The hard logic of events was forcing the issue of fiscal reform to a decision. An opportunity had presented itself in 1830 when the Wellington Ministry had been stimulated by the general economic distress to consider the radical proposals presented by Sir Henry Parnell's treatise on 'Financial Reform', which showed the existing system to be archaic and irrational and incapable of meeting either the ends of revenue or of trade. The remedy, it was argued, was a drastic reduction of customs and excise and the re-imposition of the income tax to make up for any loss of revenue. Here was the blue print of fiscal planning for *laissez-faire*, and the leaders of both parties were willing to give it a sympathetic examination, but opposition was too strong, support in the country too weak, and the proposal was dropped. The Tory government with its unpopular political views earned no merit for its enlightened fiscal views, and the torch of fiscal reform as well as that of parliamentary reform was passed to the Whigs.

Lord Althorp, the new Whig Chancellor, started with the highest intentions. 'The best way of relieving the labouring classes', he said, 'was to give them employment; and this could only be secured by reducing the taxes which pressed most immediately on the productive industry of the country.' The income tax again proved a stumbling block and all attempts to find a substitute in the form of a tax on the transfer of funded as well as landed property, and all attempts to make an inroad on the structure of the protective system, ran the gauntlet of vested interests. The Whigs missed the tide of fiscal reform in 1831 and for them it never returned. Their achievements, however, should not be forgotten. They reduced the debt charge from 4 to $3\frac{1}{2}$ per cent; they abolished the taxes on beer and inhabited houses and reduced those on paper and news-papers and removed excise on leather and printed calicoes; they also introduced the Penny Post without raising additional taxes to meet a temporary fall in post office returns. They sacrificed £7 m. of revenue and were faced with rising expenditure on the army and navy. After four successive deficits they resorted to a general increase of 5 per cent in customs and excise, but indirect taxation had reached its limits and the returns actually fell. In order to win support in the country seething with Chartist demonstrators and anti-Poor Law agitations, they promised a modification of the Corn Laws in the form of a low duty in place of the sliding scale, but however heartily the country hated the Corn Laws, it hated the Poor Law more, and the Whigs who were regarded as the authors of it were driven from power.

By 1840, the Tories had become reconciled to new direct taxa-tion to meet the deficits and to relieve the pressure of taxation on consumption: new taxation—even the income tax—was preferable to an attack on the Corn Laws which the Whigs now threatened. The way to a complete reorganization of the existing system was opened further by the Report of the Select Committee on Import Duties of 1840 which had been drawn up by the officials of the Board of Trade. It is possible, as Lucy Brown has shown in her recent study,[1] to impugn their judgement and to decry their methods, but they confirmed the strictures of Parnell on the subject of the existing tariff system by showing that 1,100 articles contributed only £360,000 to the revenue while 46 were taxed to the amount of £22,598,000; they dealt faithfully with the plea of the shipping interests that a duty of 55s. per ton on Baltic timber compared to 10s. duty on Canadian timber was necessary to keep their old ships in use for voyaging timber across the Atlantic: it was a 'form of bounty to the alms-begging shipowners as fatal in its effects', said Deacon Hume, 'as the allowance to the far more pardonable paupers'. To the officials of the Board of Trade, such forms of privilege were anathema and should be swept away, and they boldly laid down the lines of an alternative policy without waiting for the statistical apparatus which would have enabled them to plot its course. They appeared to speak with the voice of authority; and in the temper of that troubled time they must be included among the powerful agencies that impelled the Tory Party under the leadership of Sir Robert Peel to take the leap in the dark towards the most complete experiment in free trade in the history of industrial states.

Sir Robert Peel, who was returned to power in 1841, could have won the acclaim of the working classes and of many Tories by two measures: a repeal of the obnoxious 1834 Poor Law and the introduction of a Ten Hour Day. He did neither; he relieved the burdens on industry and on the standard of life by the application of the logic of the Board of Trade. Orthodox economics won its greatest victory of the century. In February 1842 he introduced a revised sliding scale designed to reduce the incentive to hoard grain and provide a more steady supply. In his budget in March he reduced duties on colonial coffee and timber and allowed the import of livestock and provisions. Modest as these measures were, they represented important changes of principle. In addition, prohibitions were swept away and duties were reduced on 750 dutiable

[1] Lucy Brown, *The Board of Trade* (1959).

articles, a measure which, it was claimed, would lower the cost of living without exposing home industries to undue competition. The expected loss of revenue was to be made up by a temporary tax of 7*d*. in the £ on incomes above £150, a proposal which was violently opposed by the Whigs and also, it may be noted, by Cobden. Revenue now rose regularly beyond the estimates and the income tax was retained so that further reductions could be made affecting coffee, currants, sugar, soap, candles, tallow, paper, starch. The vexatious excises on the various stages of glass production were swept away, and Paxton's Crystal Palace rose in 1851 as a symbol of the emancipation of that industry from fiscal bondage.

The success of Peel's experiment of pursuing social harmony through fiscal reform was recognized and applauded in most quarters; even the Chartists, who had hoped for better things, could find some virtue in it. Only the Anti-Corn Law League were dissatisfied, indeed they were alarmed: working-class support for a Tory policy boded ill for the future of radicalism, and an enlightened fiscal system might postpone rather than hasten the accomplishment of their victory over the landlords against whom they entertained a rabid hatred; to them, the Corn Laws were not only an obstacle to trade; they were a symbol of feudal privilege. The Corn Law debate was thus a reflection of social and political conflicts as well as of different interpretations of the national interest. The League aimed at scoring a victory over the hereditary ruling class and was prepared—like the middle-class reformers in 1832— to co-operate with the working class to achieve it; but whether they exercised substantial influence on the actual events is open to doubt. The success which attended Sir Robert Peel's measures appeared to confirm the League's dogmatic rejection of every vestige of protection, but Sir Robert Peel, not the League, was the true progenitor of the faith in free trade; it followed in the wake of Peelite prosperity and was strengthened, but not created, by League oratory. Sir Robert Peel was also the true author of the rapprochement between the middle and the working classes. There was no necessary connexion in his mind between the campaign for lower prices and the wage policy of employers. He had become convinced that wages did not vary with the price of provisions and stated this as one of the grounds for his conversion to repeal of the Corn Laws. League speakers were pointing out that wages were only one element in the costs of production, and that those industries in which competitive advantage was highest often paid the best wages. The subsistence theory of wages could no longer be brought forward as a barrier to an understanding between working-class leaders and free traders; and with population rising at the rate of more than 200,000 a year and British harvest fluctuations being what they were, the campaign for repeal could be presented as a race against periodical famine which only the landlords had an interest in losing. Sir Robert Peel, himself one of the most enlightened landlords in the country, was sensitive to these arguments; 'the condition of England question' was very much in his mind, and the remarkable success that attended his interim measures was a factor in persuading him that the same principle should be applied to corn as to other articles of trade. The growth of trade was increasing the revenue, the money market was so buoyant that the government was able to effect the conversion of £250 m. of the national debt—a record at that time—and the so-called Hungry Forties were mounting to the greatest mania of the century. Peel himself feared the effects of over-speculation in railways which his fiscal reform had helped to stimulate, and dreaded the consequence of a simultaneous collapse of the investment boom and a harvest failure. 'I shudder at the recurrence of such a winter and spring as those of 1841-2', he wrote to a correspondent in 1845. His fears regarding the harvest of 1845 were more than realized as a result of a wet summer which ruined the corn crop in England and the potato crop in Ireland; and the remedy, he said, 'was the removal of all impediments to the imports of all kinds of human food; that is the total and absolute repeal for ever of all duties on all articles of subsistence'. Except for a registration duty of 1s. per quarter, corn was to come in free by 1849; at the same time, the remaining protective duties on linen, cotton, and woollen manufactures were removed and the general duty of 20 per cent on foreign manufactured articles was reduced to 10 per cent, thus, as he said, applying to corn a principle of nearly universal application. 'I attach great importance to our doing, and doing now, what yet remains to be done. Let us put the finishing touch to the good work.' The 'good work' was the removal of a stumbling block not only, as he believed, to economic advance, but to national unity.

The Corn Laws were a cause of dangerous class divisions and it was part of Sir Robert's purpose to heal them.

The course of the fiscal revolution was carried a stage further by the Whig government of Lord John Russell with the repeal of the Navigation Laws in 1849 which threw the carrying trade as well as the import of corn open to all nations. The real heir of Sir Robert Peel, however, was Gladstone who, from the time of his appointment to the Board of Trade in 1841, began to exercise a growing influence which became almost a dictatorship over financial affairs. In the course of the following thirty years he completed the dismantling of the protective system by removing duties on cotton yarns and all manufactured goods and lowering and finally abolishing the duties on timber; he removed the duties on sugar and imported fruits so that food imports were now entirely free; and paper and soap were no longer subjected to excise. His principle was to tax for revenue only, with no incidental protection; to make no difference between colonial and other imports; to avoid taxation on food, such as sugar, and to concentrate on a few former luxuries that had become conventional necessities, such as tea, tobacco, alcohol; to leave the nation's wealth 'to fructify in the pockets of the people'; and above all, to help the wage-earner by freeing industry and so enhancing employment opportunities while at the same time reducing the cost of living.

The alternative to raising revenue by duties on imports was to rely on the income tax, which in Gladstone's view was more injurious than taxing the poor man's tea and tobacco. He regarded income tax as a temporary expedient to bridge the gap between the fall of revenue from tax remission and the compensating increase of revenue from rising consumption; it was a reserve in case of war or threat of war; but as a staple source of revenue it was unjust, and he refused to remove its injustice by graduating it according to the size of income since this would be a form of penalty for hard work and enterprise. He followed the lead of those—like J. S. Mill— who put their trust in inheritance taxes by subjecting real as well as personal property to a small death duty in 1853. By 1886 it produced £4 m. derived from property passing at death to the value of £140,500,000. The great tree of property had nothing to fear (though it gave a great shudder) from the axe of Gladstone.

He was much more anxious to lay his axe at the root of all evil, the National Debt. From £808 m. in 1828, it was down to £779 m. in 1885-6 in spite of the Crimean War, with tangible assets such as the telegraph system and the Suez Canal shares to set against it. In the same period the national income had risen from around £500 m. to £1,200 m., representing a rise in real income per head from perhaps £20 to £35; and between 1842-51 and 1872-81 the revenue from 1*d.* income tax had doubled. Gladstone spoke of the intoxicating plethora of wealth; the rich were getting richer and the poor less poor; and it remained a fundamental corollary of his system that money was transferred from the pockets of the consumer of tea and tobacco to the pockets of the fund holder, so that it should find its way, through the fructifying magic of the money market, once more into productive enterprise. 'Equal opportunity of becoming unequal', to adapt Professor Tawney's phrase, not equality of sacrifice, might be said to have inspired Gladstonian finance.

By 1883, the first tentative change towards the modern view of taxation was voiced by Gladstone's Chancellor, Goschen, who thought that the time had come to inquire whether the country 'does not now require a number of services which were not called for previously'; national expenditure was rising and the idea of a graduated income tax began to be favoured. By his passion for removing duties in order to stimulate trade and employment, Gladstone had defeated his own object of abolishing the income tax, and it was now available to perform the task of meeting the demand for greater economic equality which political equality had rendered ultimately beyond denial.

In the period following the repeal of the Corn Laws, British overseas trade was favoured by the mid-century boom in railway building, by iron steamship building, by rising prices, and constantly improving facilities of transport and communications. Under these circumstances, an acceleration in the rate of growth could be expected and was fully realized. In volume the rate of growth was 11 per cent per annum from 1842 to 1873 compared with 7 per cent between 1816 and 1842 and average value showed a still more striking advance, rising by 14 per cent per annum—from £50 m. to £240 m.—against a mere fraction in the period 1816-42.

The rise in value of exports was of the greatest importance in the mid-Victorian economy, and was due partly to the pressure of world demand upon the railway iron, engineering, and metal goods and other high priced products of British skill required to equip the new industrial economies of Europe and North America, and to the increased export of fully manufactured cotton goods. It also reflected a general advance of overseas purchasing power to which the growing volume of British commodity imports and capital exports substantially contributed; and associated with all these factors was the influence exerted by the gold discoveries in America and Australia. As might be expected the proportion of cotton and wool to the total fell—from 58 per cent (in value) in 1842 to 42 per cent in 1873—while the proportion of iron, coal, machinery rose from 11 to 24 per cent. In terms of value per head, exports rose from £3. 10s. to £7 between 1854 and 1872 and imports from £5. 10s. to £11, a parallel growth that reflects a favourable turn in the terms of trade. Exports were buying a relatively larger quantity of imports, and a growing proportion consisted of food, especially bacon, eggs, butter, and cheese. The British breakfast table could be supplemented more cheaply from foreign than from home supplies; and the number of those engaged in British agriculture began to fall.

The contribution of free imports to the commercial upswing cannot be measured, but it should not be exaggerated; imports, it has been noted by Professor Cairncross, rose disproportionately to any reduction in price that could be attributed to free trade; it is probable that the prospects of free import into the British market was itself a factor in the upward turn of trade, but more important than all was the advance that was being made in the mechanization of industry and in transport by land and sea, both at home and abroad. 'The industry state' had arrived in Britain, and it had definitely taken root in Europe and America where, equally divided between them, 80,000 miles of railway were laid down between 1850 and 1870. Moreover the boom was world wide and the expansion of the British market, great though it was, did not keep pace with the expansion of world exports: in 1840 British imports at £68 m. absorbed 36 per cent of the exports of all other countries; in 1873 at £305 m. the proportion was 26 per cent.

There were checks to the rate of growth in the years of the Crimean War and in the period of the Lancashire cotton famine of

1861–5; and the crisis of 1866–7 was sharp but short-lived. In the following six years all previous records were broken and large sums accrued from the balance of invisible items of exports, above all shipping services, over the deficit on merchandise account, which were left in the form of foreign investments to finance further imports and to stimulate enterprise. By 1875, they had reached a total of not less than £1,000 m., and at the height of the boom in the early 1870s were proceeding at the rate of £70 m. a year. The British market was absorbing £300 m. of the world's produce and British shipping was earning £50 m. by services all over the world. The progress of customers and competitors was assisted by the export of capital goods; £10 m. of machinery, £36 m. of iron and steel, £13 m. of coal in the boom year of 1872–3; but by far the greatest item was still cotton which at £80 m. accounted for slightly under one-third of the total of exports. The U.S.A. remained the best market but other markets were relatively more buoyant: rapid growth was stimulated by the export of capital to the Empire countries and by the industrial revolution which was now in full swing in Europe; exports to Germany rose between 1854 and 1873 from £8·5 m. to £27·3 m.; to Holland from £5,200,000 to £17,500,000, and, in spite of the Franco-Prussian War, to France from £3,200,000 to £17,400,000.

Cobden would have pointed with pride to this remarkable achievement, especially as the greatest increase occurred after the Cobden Treaty of 1860. It had been the first of a series of commercial treaties, and it included, as did most of the subsequent treaties, a 'most favoured nation clause', which had the effect of extending negotiated tariff concessions made by one country to another 'most favoured' nation, and it represents the highest achievement of the free trade spirit. Cobden believed that he had shown that 'trade was not only a law of wealth and prosperity but a law of friendship . . . a web of concord woven between people and people. This is one of the ideas made familiar to us; but permit me to remind you that it is a modern idea.' There was idealism as well as calculation in the movement for free trade.

Among the contributory causes of the fabulous advance of these years was the improvement of communications through the development of faster shipping lines and the electric cable. By this time iron had been generally adopted for steamship construction and by the end of the 1850s the iron screw steamship was taking the lead, a lead that was decisively confirmed by the service that iron screw steamers rendered in the Crimean War. Other forms of steamship construction rapidly fell behind and by 1860 the British steam merchant marine was of iron and was screw-driven. The whole steam-driven fleet represented only 10 per cent of the total British tonnage; its freight earning capacity was much greater, and by 1865, when steamships accounted for 20 per cent of the total register tonnage, they did more transport work, according to Sir John Clapham, than all the sailing ships combined. Nevertheless, even after the opening of the Suez Canal, the sailing ship retained its hold on the long hauls to the Antipodes and the Far East until the coming of the triple expansion engine in the 1880s.

The contraction of time was even more striking than that of space. In 1830, when the East Indiamen were in their prime, a message from London could be delivered in Calcutta in from five to eight months; by 1850 the overland route via Alexandria and Suez had reduced the time to a month; by 1870 the direct cable to Bombay and its extension to Singapore and Australia brought the Antipodes within a few minutes' call of London. The wool manufacturer in Yorkshire found himself in a new relationship with the grower in Australia. Still closer was the link between the Manchester cotton spinner and his source of raw material after the laying of the Atlantic cable of 1867; the long-established system by which goods were sent to England 'on consignment' in return for bills on the merchant consumed time and capital; the manufacturer was now able to send through his cotton broker firm offers to the other side before the cargo was shipped or even while it was still on the water. Buying 'of futures' became a regular feature of the cotton trade. It was denounced as a form of gambling, but merchants and brokers formed a Cotton Settlement Association in 1882 to organize the market in 'futures' and to arrange periodical cash settlements as in the market for standard securities on the Stock Exchange, and the system became an established feature of the import of staple food stuffs as well as of raw materials.

There had been a moment during the cotton famine of the early 1860s when the course of the trade in raw cotton appeared to be taking a new direction. Many observers had noted with anxiety the degree of dependence of the British cotton industry upon the U.S.A.

No less than 72 per cent of the cotton reaching British ports was American in origin and rested on the 'treacherous foundation' of slave labour. The more far-sighted merchants formed the Cotton Supply Association in 1857, and with the aid of the Foreign Office and the Consular Service—notwithstanding Lancashire's proclaimed suspicion of State action in all its forms—had been making great preparations for alternative sources of supply. The outbreak of the American Civil War confirmed their fears and India and Egypt were chosen to fulfil the role of successors to the U.S.A. Cotton seed and cotton gins were sent out in large quantities, but in spite of the famine prices which merchants were willing to pay, the proportion of Indian imports could only be raised from 19 per cent in the 1850s to 28 per cent for the period 1862-8. Egyptian supplies, though far smaller, proved more elastic; but the U.S.A. quickly resumed her leadership in cotton production after the war, and by 1880-4 she supplied nearly three-quarters of the cotton consumed in Britain.

The attempt to find imperial sources of supply to relieve the dependence of Britain on the U.S.A. is only one aspect of the close association that developed between Britain and her overseas possessions during the period of commercial imperialism. From 1850 British investments began to move from Europe to the undeveloped areas of the world, and of the £800-£1,000 m. of British foreign investment in the next twenty-five years, probably two-fifths went to British possessions. Perhaps £500 m. were in the form of government securities but most of the remainder took the form of railways, harbour installations, and the like; a very large proportion was spent on materials of British manufacture, the cost of freight in British ships, and the salaries of British engineers and managers. By 1870 nearly £100 m. of British capital had been raised for railways in India, and Indian imports of British goods rose from £9 m. to £21 m.; nearly £50 m. for railways in Australia and Canada; £8 m. in New Zealand; £2 m. in South Africa. Being long maturing investments which could not be expected to yield good returns for two or three generations, they carried a government guarantee of 5 or 6 per cent interest and were always issued at par. The *laissez-faire* state was thus giving an important stimulus to British industry while providing safe returns for British investors. At the same time the lowering of transport costs by sea and land and the increasing development of natural resources opened up by rail and steamer in the new territories caused a relative fall of price of primary products which was reflected in more favourable terms of trade for British industry between 1860 and 1872 and a substantial rise in the living standards of British workers. Returns on British capital mounted steadily from £12 m. per annum in the early 1850s to over £50 m. in the early 1870s. A striking—and as events were to prove—a welcome reinforcement of the balance of payments was thus being made and British exporters as well as investors were reaping a rich harvest; it is true that interest rates at home were kept up and colonial taxation grew to meet the debt charges; but against these must be set the opening up of vast new territories for white settlement and development and the unification of the Indian sub-continent.

By the late 1870s, the situation was no longer so favourable to Britain. She was now importing half her meat, wool, and dairy produce and more than half her corn. She was wholly dependent on imports for her cottons, and the import of Spanish haematite iron for conversion into steel rose by 1882 to over 3 million tons. At the same time, her export trade was relatively stagnant. From a peak of £256 m. in 1872 it fell to less than £200 m. in the three black years 1877–9 and averaged scarcely £230 m. at current values for the next ten years. These values reflect an unfavourable turn in the terms of trade as well as a fall in the rate of growth: between 1873 and 1883 exports rose in volume by 34 per cent and imports by 38 per cent, but in value exports fell by 6 per cent while imports rose by 14 per cent. A negative balance on trade and services taken together began to show itself, and it was fortunate that the income of previous foreign investment was available to meet it. A positive balance of £24·6 m. on services and merchandise between 1871 and 1875 was turned into a negative balance of £31·5 m. between 1876 and 1880, but a return of £56·3 m. on interest and dividends left a net balance of £24·9 m.

What is the reason for the setback of the late 1870s? Distinguished contemporaries sometimes attributed it to complacency on the part of masters and men after a generation of quasi-monopoly of the world's market; they expected to live more luxuriously than their competitors, it was said; industrial management was passing slowly—perhaps too slowly—from the age of rugged individualists to salaried directors of limited companies; there is some evidence of entrepreneurial weakness in the development of steel and electricity; and it is certain that technical education in Britain lagged behind that of her competitors. But the most potent factor was the rise of foreign competitors whose spectacular race to maturity had been made possible by Britain herself. Moreover they were in no mood to dally with the abstract arguments of the Manchester school which ran counter to the forces of nationalism and affronted powerful vested interests, especially after the triumph of Germany over France and of the American manufacturing North over the cotton-growing South.

In 1872 France denounced the Cobden Treaty, and the keystone of the international system of liberal tariffs gave way; only the most favoured nation clause remained. Between 1879 and 1885, the tide of free trade ebbed rapidly and tariff walls began to rise in most European countries almost to the heights of the pre-1860 era. The British self-governing territories overseas also began to protect their infant industries and the United States built around herself a barrier of duties ranging from 35 to 100 per cent *ad valorem*. The British market itself began to be invaded: iron and steel goods, chemicals and laboratory appliances, nursery toys and cheap cutlery, began to raise the problem of things 'made in Germany', and the heavy balance of imports over exports began to give rise to discussion tinged with anxiety. Was British prosperity on the decline? Were free imports necessarily the same thing as free trade? The calculations of Sir Robert Giffen reassured those who were worried by the enormous excess of imports; he showed that the adverse balance of payments was being met, not by the sale of foreign investments, but by the invisible earnings of investments, shipping, banking, insurance, and the short term credits of commercial services. The 'Fair Traders' with their suggestions for low tariffs on manufactures and non-empire food products were swamped by the tide of urban resentment at any suggestion of interfering with the cheap loaf.

But the case for free imports rested on a much sounder foundation; Britain's free trade policy enabled other industrial powers to find an outlet for their goods without having to intensify the competition in Britain's overseas markets. So long as Britain could find money to pay the mounting deficit on the trade account, her rivals had no strong incentive to force their manufactured goods on to the markets which supplied them with food and raw materials. Britain was able to perform this enormous task by her 'invisible' earnings, and also by the flexibility with which she was able to switch her export of capital and reduce the deficit in one area of exchange by developing a balance in another. Thus, in 1872–8, while exports of iron, steel, and tinplates to the U.S.A. declined to little more than one-sixth, those to India and Australia rose by nearly 150 per cent; cotton exports to Empire countries, especially to India, continued to expand between 1872 and 1879 when they were falling in nearly every other market.[1] At the same time, while foreign borrowing declined, Empire borrowing rose—£40 m. to Australia between 1873 and 1879 and probably the same to India—and the share of British exports going to Empire markets rose between 1871 and 1877 from 23 to 35·1 per cent. These markets were largely insulated from the effects of the depression through their export of essential raw material and food products, and by the export of British capital for the development of railways. At the same time Britain was herself a large exporter of primary products in the form of coal and re-exported Australian wool which enabled her to build up credit balances with other industrial countries for multilateral settlement of accounts.

The close relation with Empire countries had penalties as well as privileges: the free access to the Indian market encouraged a dangerous concentration on cotton production and postponed the effort to diversify the output of British industry; investment tended to follow beaten paths rather than to challenge the U.S.A. and Germany for the leadership of the new industries, and the manifest signs of a slowing down in the rate of growth of industrial production and productivity in the basic industries stimulated a debate that still goes on. Was entrepreneurial lassitude to blame for the changed tempo of British economic growth? Or was it that the stagnation in the export trade discouraged investment in new enterprises? The temporary cessation of foreign lending after the shock of 1873 also had a depressing effect by reducing foreign purchasing power, but capital exports were resumed in the 1880s. Whatever the reasons may have been, world trade in manufactures

[1] See S. B. Saul, *Studies in British Overseas Trade 1870–1914* (1960), Ch. VI.

grew more slowly during the Great Depression than before,[1] and Britain's share of it actually declined. Britain's answer was to turn more and more to Empire and non-protected markets while maintaining her own free market. By these means she was able to perform her role as the pivot in the international settlement of accounts, a role of inestimable value at a time when falling prices might have turned back the faltering tide of international co-operation behind the walls of intensified economic nationalism. British agriculture suffered in the process, but owing to its historic flexibility and its natural advantages, the sacrifice was not greater than it could bear.

[1] See Musson, op. cit., and p. 45 above.

5

Banking, Credit, and Joint-Stock Enterprise

IN A COUNTRY so rich as Britain, with a ruling class of mercantile habit of mind and often of mercantile origin, the existence of adequate resources for investment was never in doubt. The problem of capital supply lay in the growth of self-regulating agencies by which the savings of those in possession of a surplus could be made available to those in need of capital for their current and long-term transactions. The organs for the transference of funds from areas of surplus to areas of deficiency had grown in answer to the expanding needs of trade and industry, an example of the disposition which British people had to an outstanding degree for taking legitimate risks in the hope of gain; but the mechanism of exchange was wholly unplanned, and by the second quarter of the nineteenth century the question of whether it would prove itself susceptible to rational control had become a matter of urgency.

Perhaps the most vulnerable—yet indispensable—link in the chain was that of the country banks. They were, for the most part, country banks in reality as well as in name, the creation of local corn-dealers, cattle-drovers, wool-staplers, and the new manufacturers, whose chief function it was to discount local bills and so provide currency in the form of country bank notes to fill the ever-widening gap between the means of payment and the inelastic supply of coin. Some industrial areas, as a result of painful experience of the frailty of country banks, preferred to have their currency in the form of bills of exchange. Lancashire used coin or notes for wages, but almost all other transactions were settled by the exchange of bills and promissory notes; they also formed a great part of the currency of the West Riding, Cheshire, Shropshire, and Derby-shire; they passed from hand to hand and rested for their credit worthiness on the confidence which each holder placed on previous assignors; in the country as a whole, the aggregate of such bills might represent more than all the notes and guineas circulating at any time.

The inland bill had arisen out of the ordinary transactions of merchants and had existed long before the appearance of country banks. With the growth in the volume of inland trade it had come to play an essential part in the settlement of accounts; a bill drawn on a London firm of repute would pass almost any-where in the country; and the discounting system which grew up around it represented an adaptation to a particular set of circumstances which was frequently imitated but never fully reproduced in any other part of the world. It sprang from the necessities of the small country banks of the agricultural part of the country to find an outlet for their surplus funds through an intermediary in London—a bill broker—who used their cash to discount bills of the 'industrial' banks of the west and the Midlands. As Bagehot said, 'localization was the cause of that wonderful superfluity of money we have in London'; and with the rapid multiplication of banks in the early nineteenth century, and the increasing necessity for finding fresh outlets for surplus funds, the country banks came to rely more and more on the professional broker for this service.

Not less important was the web of credit through which the transactions of foreign trade were conducted. The enormous import of cotton in the last quarter of the eighteenth century called for the development of a specialized agency—the cotton broker—to act as intermediary between the importer and the manufacturer. Quite frequently, the broker advanced credit to the importer by paying freight, import dues, and insurance as an advance against sales, perhaps months before final disposal of the consign-ment. The broker thus established himself as an essential link between the importer and the market, and a strong feeling of confidence grew up between them. The buyer's dependence on the broker was established by 1800, and Edward Baines, the historian of the industry, spoke in 1835 'of the strict probity and honour' invariably associated with the Liverpool cotton broker, 'enabling an enormous business' to be conducted 'with a facility and despatch which have no parallel in any market in the world'.

At the heart of the export trade was the commission agent, who consigned goods to the importer overseas for whom he acted and in addition allowed the suppliers of the goods to draw a bill on himself to an amount of about two-thirds or three-quarters of the shipment. The importer would be given from three to six months' credit or even longer, and the manufacturer, having drawn the bill on the commission agent and having had it accepted by him, would turn it into cash through the discount market. Large firms took the risk of merchanting themselves and produced to the order of their overseas customers. Import trade with the less developed markets, especially the market in food supplies and raw materials, called for credit advances at every step of the way; coffee, sugar, corn were consigned to London, bills were drawn on the consignee at once and he would dispose of the produce as opportunity offered, sometimes holding it for months or even for years. Where the goods originated in plantations which were mortgaged to British merchants, as in the case of the West Indies, the standing of the original owner would be known and the advance would be made against known assets; but even where this was not the case, 'the usual rather blind advances were made'; a necessary risk, says Sir John Clapham, of new trading with countries recently opened up, and a great convenience in the 'gigantic produce trade' with impecunious Ireland. Several large merchant firms became accepting houses; they lent their names to importers and accepted bills drawn against consignments from abroad, so rendering the bills much more marketable, and by their knowledge of the parties concerned, facilitated and safeguarded the whole course of trade. Overend Gurney and Co. described themselves as bill brokers and bankers; Timothy Wiggin started as a Manchester export merchant but described himself as a banker whose work was to 'accept bills drawn abroad and receive' bills remitted from various parts of the world to meet payment of them.

The mechanism of commercial exchange on the whole worked well; it must be regarded as one of the major contrivances that have brought about the modern world and as a great tribute to the British empirical tradition; but it depended for its smooth operation on a stable international currency, and the fulfilment of this condition represented one of the most intractable of the problems of the early age of industrialism.

As a result of the post-war fall of prices—partly occasioned by the government's return to cash payments between 1819 and 1821— debtors found they were paying more in real values than they had borrowed, and such diverse authorities as the economist Ricardo and the poet Shelley were at one in advocating a national levy to pay off the National Debt once and for all. The charge on the debt fell from the peak figure of £32 m. in 1816 to £28 m. in 1830, but prices had fallen relatively faster, i.e. by 28 per cent; foreign trade was meeting the resistance of tariffs and such gains as the working class were making as a result of falling prices were off-set for many of them by unemployment; tithes and long leases were becoming more burdensome to farmers, and parsons and fund-holders appeared to be reaping where they had not sown. Cobbett's attacks on Jews and stock jobbers and such similar organisms as infested the Great Wen had a wide and sympathetic hearing. His remedy was to return to gold but to repudiate all claims made since the inauguration of the paper pound in 1797; Thomas Attwood, the Birmingham banker, wanted to manage the currency by buying gold at a price which would ensure full employment and general prosperity; but he never explained how he would keep this induced inflation under control. The government had already decided (as the act of 1821 shows) that the chief cause of fluctuation was the volume of the note issue and that the best way of ensuring stability was to make notes convertible for gold at pre-war parity. At the same time, they did something to reduce the burden of the debt charge by effecting the conversion of £150 m. of debt from 5 to 4 per cent which helped to stimulate a 'restless feeling and a disposition to hazardous investments' culminating in the speculative boom of 1825-6.

The collapse of 1825-6 made it plain that a convertible currency was as capable as any other of being issued in excess and of bringing about a commercial cataclysm; and though the Bank of England by no means escaped criticism, the finger of accusation was pointed at the country banks. Seventy-two of them, south of the Border, had gone down in the crash, whereas only one of the joint-stock banks of Scotland had failed, the first in forty years.

As a first step to control the note issue, both the Bank of England and the remaining 300 country banks lost the right to issue notes under £5 by the Act of 1826. It was presumed that gold would take their place and so increase the reserve in the pockets of the people; but whether this tacit reserve would grow in proportion to the cheques and bills and bank loans was not considered, since these were not regarded as 'money' or 'currency' but as its substitute; the level of prices, it was assumed, depended solely on the quantity of notes and coin in circulation. The relative immunity of Scotland from bank failures underlined the weakness of the English private banks and gave the friends of joint-stock banking the confidence to challenge the monopoly of the Bank of England. By the Bank Act of 1826 joint-stock banks could be formed outside a radius of sixty-five miles of London, and the Bank of England was pointedly invited to exercise its power to form branches; by the Act of 1833 joint-stock banks could be formed anywhere, including London itself, though the London joint-stock banks were not to issue notes.

The Bank of England branches did not merely issue notes; they discounted bills at London rates, which were somewhat lower than country rates; but they refused to allow overdrafts and gave no interest on long deposits. They proved to be less of a menace than the private banks had feared, and they came to be accepted by them as stabilizing influences. The joint-stock banks had a far greater impact; by 1836 there were seventy-nine issuing their own notes and twenty (mainly in London) which did not issue. They were the result of keen local enterprise and they went out for business in a way that shocked the old 'gentleman bankers'. The great expansion of cotton, iron, and railway enterprise which came to a climax in 1836 owed not a little to the complacency with which the joint-stock banks met requests—or indeed, invited them—for long-term as well as short-term advances, and replenished their supplies of cash by re-discounting bills on the London discount market without inquiring too closely about the standing of those on whom they were originally drawn. They carried the wave of optimism into all parts of the country and the country banks were drawn reluctantly in their turbulent wake.

Two interlocking lines of policy can thus be distinguished: the centralizing of the note issue and the strengthening of the bank structure by the establishment of branch banks and joint-stock

D

banks. A third question had to be faced: the management of its own note issue by the Bank itself, torn as it was between its half-realized obligations as a central bank and its still lively awareness of the expectations of its shareholders. It was blamed for advancing money to Government in connexion with the payment of army pensions and so contributing to the over-supply of money; by effecting the conversion of 1823-4 it was said to have stimulated the boom in company issues; and by its own participation in the discount market it had contributed to the supply of credit—and the enhancement of its own profits—at a time when restriction rather than expansion was needed. It is possible to find excuses on all these counts, but that something was due to its critics seems to be implied by its recognition of the 'Palmer rules'—after Horsley Palmer who first enunciated them in 1832—of withdrawing in normal times from competition in the discount market and of holding long term securities at a fixed level while allowing notes to fluctuate up and down according to the level of bullion, the level to be held at about one-third of its liabilities. The notes were now expected to behave in all respects like gold; and Horsley Palmer provided a prescient hint of how this rigidity might be mitigated by recommending that in times of stress, the Bank should discount approved bills *ad libitum* but at a rate higher than the market rate.

That this recommendation was seriously meant is implied by the provision of the Act of 1833 that the Bank should be allowed to raise the rate of discount for bills at three months at its discretion. But it was one thing to recognize the basic principles of central banking and another to apply them, in view of the expectation of the shareholders of the Bank that it should make a profit, like any other bank, and, more especially, in view of the tendency on the part of the leading authorities—the Currency School as they came to be called from 1840—to identify currency with notes and coin and to ignore money in the form of credit. The gold standard mechanism was, therefore, left as the automatic regulator: it would bring about an exchange of notes for gold when prices were too high and the foreign exchanges were adverse. Gold would leave the country and the note issue would fall; prices would fall as the note issue fell, exports would rise and imports would fall and the gold would return. But, as Thomas Tooke, the leader of the opposing school of thought—the Banking School—pointed out, there was nothing to prevent other agencies, e.g. the private and joint-stock banks, from filling the gap—or the Bank itself from forgetting its own rule and increasing its own discounts, as indeed it did in the first six months of 1836. And all the time the practice of obtaining overdrafts and drawing cheques was spreading and increasing the work of the bankers' clearing houses through which immense payments were made without the use of a negotiable instrument at all.

The prosperity of 1834-6 fed upon all these sources of credit, and when the reaction came in 1837, owing to external causes as well as to excessive speculation at home, the Bank again came under heavy fire. It was charged with lending money which had been deposited with it from the loan to the West Indian slave-owners (under the slave emancipation agreement) and by the East India Company. Horsley Palmer's reply to the criticism is significant: 'It never could be expected that the Bank should be required to pay interest for notes or bullion to others merely for the sake of keeping them unemployed.' At a time of expansion, this is just what the Bank, in the view of its critics, should have done in order to protect its reserves. The private and public responsibilities of the Bank were again shown to be in conflict.

The main pressure upon the reserve, however, came from the collapse of the American boom, which the Bank itself was accused of having encouraged by a low bank rate. When the crisis was upon it in the autumn of 1836, it raised the rate to 4 per cent, then to 5 per cent, and refused to discount any bill which already bore the signature of a joint-stock bank. When the effects of restriction were seen to be reaching crisis proportions, the Bank switched to expansion, came to the rescue of firms in distress, and helped to stem the tide of disaster, but not to allay the rising temper of the business community. As the crisis subsided, gold flowed back and the Bank lowered its rate again to 4 per cent and actually sent £1 m. of gold to support American interests with which many British firms were interlocked; but a collapse of prices on the Continent and the large-scale purchase of grain owing to the worst harvest for thirty years caused a renewal of the drain and by 6 August 1839 the bank rate was raised to 6 per cent.

By this time the Manchester merchants could contain their wrath no longer, and in an outspoken pamphlet they charged the Bank with sacrificing the stability of the country to its own selfish interests by overlending and so increasing its own profits at the expense of the reserve. They estimated that £40 m. had been lost through the collapse of prices in 1837 and a further fall had taken place in 1839. The manufacturing interest could not withstand such stupendous fluctuations which had brought to 'some of the most prudent and wealthy of our merchants and manufacturers . . . that ruin which in a more wholesome and natural state of the circulating medium, could befall only the reckless adventurer and gambler'.

The indignation of the Manchester merchants did less than justice to the Bank's difficulties, especially those of 1839 when a loss of £10 m. of gold in exchange for corn and a loan of £2 m. from the Bank of France were the only alternatives to famine. Certainly, the 'Palmer rules' had broken down: the Bank had not kept out of the ordinary discount market; it had failed to maintain a fixed level of securities; the circulation had been allowed to get out of step with bullion, and the bank rate had been raised too slowly and lowered too quickly for the safety of the reserve. The Bank had obviously not reached full stature: it was both a profit-making concern and a public institution with enormous responsibilities, but it was half-hearted about exercising them. In the inquiry which followed it is by no means certain that any individual or group had a clear view of the path that lay ahead, and the decision of the government under the influence of the Currency School was perhaps as good as any available alternative. Since the Currency School—in opposition to the Banking School—believed that the note issue had a direct effect on the level of domestic prices, and that outflows of gold caused by excessive imports could be checked by contracting the note issue and so lowering prices and encouraging exports, the key to price stability lay in tying the note issue still more closely to gold. In order to effect this the Bank, by the Act of 1844, was divided into two departments, the Issue Department, which alone had the right to issue notes, and the Banking Department, which was left to conduct its affairs like any other bank. The number of notes to be issued was not to exceed £14 m. against securities (the fiduciary issue) and as many more as there was bullion to cover them. The note issue was to vary automatically pound for pound with the gold reserve; and the centralization of the note issue was brought sensibly nearer by the provisions that no new banks of issue were to be formed and the existing ones were not to increase their issue beyond the average for the last three months preceding the Act; the banks which for any reason ceased to issue should forfeit the right to issue at any future time. The Currency School expected great things of the Act: 'it will effectively prevent the recurrence of those cycles of commercial excitement and depression that our ill regulated currency has been the primary cause of', said their spokesman, Colonel Torrens.

He was quickly undeceived; within three years the nation was in the throes of a commercial crisis that threatened to reach the proportions of that of 1825-6, and the Banking Department was held to have contributed to it by re-entering the discount market and to have encouraged railway speculation by lowering its discount rate to $2\frac{1}{2}$ per cent. In October 1845, share prices of the new railway companies collapsed and there was panic among those who had to find the money to meet the calls on the shares they had bought for speculation. A second blow fell with the need to import corn to meet the bad harvest of 1847. The Bank's reserves began to fall. The rate of interest rose from 3 to $3\frac{1}{2}$ per cent, to 4 and 5 and 6 per cent on some bills; many were rejected altogether. Railway companies came into the market for funds at any price in order to finish their projects. By October, panic reigned and a deputation of London bankers went to the Government to petition for relief by a suspension of the Bank Charter Act. The fears that the source of credit would dry up with the disappearance of the gold reserve were dispelled when the Government promised an indemnity should the Directors of the Bank of England find it necessary to issue beyond the legal limit; but they made it a condition that a rate of 8 per cent should be charged to keep the borrowing within bounds. The panic thereupon subsided.

The deterrent effect of a high bank rate and the encouraging effect of a promise to lend—at a price—had at last been brought together by force of circumstances as the two-edged instrument of credit control; but the lesson of how and when to use it had still to be learned. On two further occasions—1857 and 1866[1]—the Bank was released from the restrictions imposed on it under the Act of 1844. The disturbances of the Crimean War and the speculation arising from the American gold discoveries caused a drain in 1856

[1] See below, pp. 111-12.

which appeared to have been adequately met by a raising of the bank rate to 7 per cent; but whether the Bank was itself entirely guiltless of encouraging the speculative movement by its dealings in the discount market was still in debate when the real blow fell. The speculative blizzard which swept America in 1857 brought down a number of famous British houses, especially in Scotland, where the savings of many humble depositors were involved in the suspension of payment by the Western and City of Glasgow banks. Gold left London, the reserve fell to £1½ m., and again the 1844 Act was suspended to enable the Bank to lend beyond the legal fiduciary issue. On this occasion, the statutory limit was actually exceeded by £2 m. and confidence was gradually restored. The Bank now admitted that it was part of its duty to 'control evil tendencies in their beginning'; it began to recognize that a fall in the reserve should be taken as a warning signal that anticipatory measures were necessary; moreover, the international responsibilities of the Bank were growing and the movements of gold in other parts of the world as well as the purely domestic situation had to be taken into account. The bank rate was therefore made to fluctuate widely and frequently in attempts to keep the market rates steady, and between 1860 and 1865 there were sixty changes ranging between 2 and 9 per cent, but, in the interests of its shareholders, the Bank had still not withdrawn entirely from the bill market.

The panic of 1866 raised the question of the Bank's public and private responsibilities in a more acute form. It was essentially a speculators' crisis and it left the main structure of banking unaffected, but again the Bank was authorized to exceed the statutory issue at a 10 per cent bank rate if the need should arise. The more important question of whether the Bank, by participating in the discount market, had stimulated speculation, had again to be met, and the necessity of sacrificing its discount business in the public interest was now finally faced. In 1878, the Bank announced that henceforth, however large its reserve, money would not be available *ad libitum* at market rate except to its regular customers. To everyone else, accommodation would be available at the bank rate (which was usually higher than the market rate), a decision which the Bank began to manipulate in such a way as to acquire a paramount influence on the rates for short-term loans in the London money market, and therefore in the money markets of the world.

This was all the more important since the bill of exchange was becoming more and more the medium of international, as distinct from domestic, trade where it was no longer necessary owing to the rapid growth of regional joint-stock banking, and bills flowed from every part of the world to the centre where gold could always be obtained on demand. Foreign banks were opening offices in London in the 1870s at the headquarters of the world's gold supply, and acquiring almost a monopoly of the foreign exchange business. The famous houses of Rothschild and Baring which had long concentrated on the issuing and accepting of foreign loans were joined by representatives of foreign merchant bankers who were now turning to international finance; the committee of the London Stock Exchange which had started in 1802 for the regulation of business in English stocks had become an international body which could—and did—refuse quotation of foreign government loans; Lloyd's marine insurance had its network of agencies 'over the whole earth', and its accepted criterion of security—'A1 at Lloyd's' —had become part of common speech. London was the world's banker, and at a time when British industrial supremacy was being challenged in Europe and America, the Old Lady of Threadneedle Street was extending her benign influence in all parts of the world.

In the meantime the men in charge of the day-to-day conduct of economic operations were finding capital as and where they could and making decisions involving future commitments of resources in the twilight of limited knowledge and entrepreneurial instinct. There were only limited opportunities of tapping the supplies of blind capital through the market in shares, though this was steadily becoming a practical possibility after the successful completion of the canal network and the beginning of railways. Until the joint-stock companies emerged from the restrictions of the Bubble Act of 1720, entrepreneurs continued to enlarge their capital by ploughing back profits, including sometimes even the interest on capital; or they took a new partner, unpopular though this was, since it implied sharing responsibility; and it was characteristic of enterprise at this time that ownership and control should go as closely together as possible, preferably in the same person. Or they might raise loans on the security of bond or mortgage. With the increase of middle-class and landlords' savings (often from the income derived from leases of coal and iron resources) the amount of capital from this source grew, but there was danger as well as convenience in having too easy recourse to it. Overheads tended to mount, and when sales fell off the burden of debt might be too heavy. Another source was the banks. Both before and still more after the growth of joint-stock banking, the supply of long-term as well as short-term advances of bank capital was an important factor in industrial growth. The Bank of England made loans to iron-masters after the Napoleonic Wars and it financed South Wales iron-masters through its branches after 1826; the new joint-stock banks assisted the haematite iron companies of Cumberland, and Bessemer had the support of bank loans in launching the 'converter' at Sheffield. The weakness of local banks remained a serious embarrassment, and employers might find their operations brought to a stand by the failure of local supplies of credit for wages and day-to-day transactions. Relief was sometimes given by the larger employers, who drew on the local banks for currency only after paying in an equivalent sum or making it available through their agents in London or other large towns; and the establishment of Bank of England branches and joint-stock banks, and the amalgamation of local banks, brought further strength to the credit system. The domination of the impersonal capital market was still some way off, and the personal element continued to remain the most important factor governing the flow of funds for investment. The laws of bankruptcy were such as to forbid the growth of a single market for risk-bearing capital; while an investor had to expose the whole of his property to the risks of a concern over which he had little or no control, his only safeguard was the known character of those who were responsible for its management. 'Without [sic] I was sole controlling manager', said William Crawshay, 'I would not be a partner in the Bank of England if my whole property was liable.'[1]

The railways were the chief agent in breaking down the barriers of the free flow of capital. They attracted blind capital to themselves and stimulated its attraction in others. Between 1830 and 1850 nearly a score of iron companies in Wales alone issued prospectuses in the wake of the railway booms of 1836 and 1845 and drew responses from Yorkshire cloth manufacturers, West of

[1] See also A. H. John, *The Industrial Development of South Wales 1750–1850*, for the problem of entrepreneurial investments.

England yeomen, servants, spinsters. The capital market had moved a significant stage further towards its full development, and the coming of limited liability in the next decade signalized a new phase in its evolution.

Britain, the home of *laissez-faire*, was singularly loth to extend the logic of freedom to the field of investment. From the time of the Bubble Act of 1720, joint-stock enterprise had been kept under watchful restraint, and the monopoly of the Bank of England had prevented its extension to the one field of enterprise, private banking, where its virtues had been most fully demonstrated in the banking experience of Scotland. British industry and English banking were built up under the law of partnership by which the individual partners were responsible to their last penny for the debts of the concern; and since responsibility was personal, so was direction and management. The reality was not quite so rigid as it is made to sound. Unincorporated companies could obtain some protection under the law of equity and even obtain a degree of limited liability for their shareholders (notably in the field of insurance) provided that they inscribed the fact in contracts with outside parties. Shares in such concerns came to be called 'equities', the name by which ordinary shares are known today; but in the eye of the common law all concerns other than the incorporated companies were partnerships, mere collections of individuals. In showing such reluctance to extend the principle of limited liability to joint-stock investment, Britain appeared to lag behind her neighbours abroad, but in fact, owing to the wide diffusion of capital throughout the country and the responsiveness of capitalists of all social classes to economic opportunity, the absence of limited liability was not a bar to investment even in the largest enterprises —far larger than in countries, e.g. France, where the law was in advance of that of England; and alongside the traditional partnerships consisting usually of friends and their friends, joint-stock companies of shareholders were coming into existence with or without limited liability and in spite of the law.

In 1825 the Bubble Act of 1720 was repealed and it was no longer illegal to form joint-stock companies with transferable shares; but the fate of many of the newly formed companies appeared to be such as to confirm the fears of those who identified joint-stock flotation with irresponsibility merging into deliberate fraud. Of the 624 companies that had been floated in 1824-5 only 127 continued to exist in 1827 but there were still 156 companies formed before 1824 mainly consisting of public utilities—gas, water, canal, harbour installations, insurance, and Scottish banks—and it was widely believed that the experience of 1824-5 had cured the speculative fever for joint-stock enterprise outside the range of enterprise of this kind.

What was the legal standing of these companies? Alongside those which had acquired 'power of suit' and limited liability by virtue of their corporate status through the possession of a Royal Charter or by the passage of a private act which conferred parallel privileges, there were many successful quasi-corporations which maintained an active existence (in spite of the opposition of the common lawyers) largely by reason of the fact that it was not practicable for creditors to pursue the poorer shareholders in the event of failure. There was vigorous discussion of the problem of the limitation of liability, but it centred, not on the general limitation of liability which few advocated, but upon the virtues of differential limitation such as obtained in France, where the ordinary shareholders or sleeping partners enjoyed limited liability but the managing partners were still liable to their last penny. In 1834 the fever of speculation broke out again and pleas were made for the recognition of limited liability for those companies, including banks, which fulfilled two essential conditions: namely, fully paid up capital and entire publicity of accounting. 'No,' said *The Times*, referring especially to the banks, 'it is to wealthy shareholders that the public looks for security; limit this liability and the bank becomes a delusion'; and McCulloch thought that the proposal would go far 'to annihilate whatever there is of solidity in the present system'. The tide of blind capital continued to rise, however, and the immense expansion of railway capital under joint-stock management gave the signal for a burst of imitators with or without limitation of liability. In 1834-6 companies were promoted with a total nominal capital of £135 m.; many of them arose in connexion with mining and some with iron smelting. There were also twenty-four corporately owned woollen mills in the West Riding, of highly dubious legal status, but—in spite of limited concessions in 1834 and 1837—the general regulation of joint-stock enterprise was still delayed. However, the advance of joint-stock investment continued mainly in mining, shipping, insurance, gas, and water companies. Many bore a dubious character and investors suffered heavy losses; and after an inquiry by a committee under the chairmanship of Mr. Gladstone, the Joint Stock Companies Registration Act was passed in 1844 which laid down certain conditions for full regulation: in particular, half-yearly returns of members and their holdings; the appointment of auditors and the publication of an annual balance sheet. Their shortcomings were to be subjected to 'the wholesome remedy of public opinion', and though the unincorporated company was at last recognized by the law it was not granted limited liability as a matter of general right.

As in 1824-5, and in 1836, so again in 1844 the returning tide of prosperity was signalized by a flood of new joint-stock ventures. Interest rates were low; deposits were accumulating and capital was seeking fresh outlets after the long depression. Moreover, owing to the good harvests of 1843-4, prices were low and the working classes had a surplus with which to make up their savings exhausted during the lean years since 1837. There were many thousands of friendly societies, over a million depositors in savings banks, and over 2,000 building societies with an aggregate annual income of £2,400,000. Where were their savings to go? The public debt was diminishing, and in any case investors were becoming dissatisfied with the 'sweet simplicity of the three per cents'. The laws of partnership inhibited the small investor from investing in industrial undertakings, yet public services like waterworks, bath and wash houses, gas undertakings, were held up for lack of capital because no convenient channel existed to connect the supply with the demand. Working men, it was declared, had a *right* to have a properly safe-guarded medium of investment for their savings: they should be able to form joint-stock companies 'to increase wealth by the profits of their own consumption', said a member of the Nottingham Co-operative Society in 1840.

The subject was taken up by the Christian Socialists as a means of bridging the gulf that was dividing rich and poor. They complained that investment in socially useful projects in which working men might put their savings was being held up owing to the prohibitive charges made by the Board of Trade for incorporation, and the case of the Company for Metropolitan Model Lodging Houses for Working Men, which obtained its charter only after a payment of £1,100 mainly in the form of fees to the law officers of the Crown, gave point to the argument. Co-operation was in the air, especially in the neighbourhood of Rochdale and Oldham, and though the Christian Socialists were mistaken in thinking that limited liability would open the way to a significant degree of working-class participation in industry, there is no doubt that they made a substantial contribution to the movement which culminated in the Acts of 1855, 1856, 1857, and 1862 by which general limited liability became available for all types of enterprise. The pressure had come, not from industry or the professional money market, but from reformist organizations and above all from the small provincial investors who were numerous and strong enough to press their claim to a share in the profits of enterprise over which they had neither the power nor the wish to exercise control.

By 1862 limited liability had been extended to any seven persons upon registration of association according to the procedure established in 1844, but many joint-stock banks declined to take advantage of it until they were taught their lesson by the collapse of the City of Glasgow Bank in 1878. Reliance was placed upon the advance of accounting and auditing which, as a result of the establishment of chartered associations in Edinburgh and other commercial centres from 1834, now achieved a professional status, and care was taken that auditing should become a reality. Between 1856 and 1862 almost 2,500 companies were incorporated with limited liability, and after the passing in 1862 of the act providing for general limited liability, there was a further registration of over 3,000 companies between 1862 and 1866, but of these nearly one-third failed to materialize. A number of them consisted of finance companies concentrating on short-term commercial loans, the negotiation of foreign concessions, and the promotion of railways abroad. Fifty such companies were offering shares to the public between 1862 and 1867 and helping to swell the volume of speculation to the level of mania in the crisis year of 1866.

A far more significant feature was the extension of limited liability to manufacturing and trading concerns, including iron, steel, and textiles, most notable of which were the famous Oldham mills financed by the operatives and managed by boards of directors responsible to them.[1] Many existing partnerships were converted to joint-stock form, and boards of directors began to take the place of individual heads of well-known firms, especially in iron and coal, banking, shipping, and building. They were sometimes no more than screens for notorious frauds but, as the mass of unpaid-up capital became absorbed or disappeared with the collapse of the worst companies, the evils of reckless speculation and fraud began to decline; British banking henceforth eschewed speculative promotion of all kinds, and the acceptance of general limited liability came to be associated with a rise rather than a fall in commercial morality.

It was also associated with a growth in the size of the industrial unit, especially in iron and shipbuilding where old firms such as Ebbw Vale, Bolckow and Vaughan, John Brown, Cammell Laird quickly adopted company organization. Other famous firms— Lowthian Bell, Joseph Whitworth, Nettlefolds—became private companies, but very large segments of industry were still in private hands and knew nothing of joint-stock organization for many years. Amalgamation for the purpose of market control was made easier but not inevitable by the spread of joint-stock forms of organization, and the familiar figure of the captain of industry who took the chief risk and shouldered corresponding responsibility did not immediately pass from the scene. The divorce between ownership and control and the rise of the paid manager subject to an anonymous and largely absentee board of directors marked the end of the heroic age of enterprise, and the spread of the transferable share as the most widely held form of property diffused the rights of ownership over a wide class of *rentiers*. The degree of diffusion, however, can be exaggerated; and in the light of the history of famous firms of the late nineteenth century, reflecting in their meteoric rise the energy and imagination of outstanding individuals, the break with the past was neither as complete nor as sudden as some accounts would suggest, and the qualities of the pioneers reasserted themselves through the medium of joint-stock organization.

The newer consumption industries catering for the expanding mass market provide some striking examples: ready-made clothes, boots and shoes, newspapers, and patent medicines. Cheap foreign food brought opportunities for brilliant entrepreneurial

[1] See above, p. 25.

improvisation from which firms like those of Joseph Lyons and Thomas Lipton, Cadbury, and Rowntree rose to eminence. Falling prices of raw materials and rising demand for better conditions of life by a population that was growing faster than ever before brought new types of enterprise and a new class of entrepreneurs which collectively go far to refute the charges of entrepreneurial weakness that have sometimes been made as the underlying cause of the so-called Great Depression. Such names as Lever and Beecham, Newnes and Northcliffe, Guinness and Courtauld, Ludwig Mond and Dorman Long show that the springs of enterprise were running as freely as ever. 'These and scores of others extended the scope of entrepreneurship far beyond the frontiers of pig iron and cotton stockings which still seem to bar its understanding to some who write about it.'[1]

If there was entrepreneurial weakness, it was usually in the older branches of industry, especially in iron manufacture, where economies of scale were of the first importance in meeting the challenge from abroad. Here the family firm, whatever the form of its organization, proved that it had outlived its usefulness, and its struggle for survival must be included among the causes of the inefficiency with which British industry was charged.

[1] See Charles Wilson, 'Economy and Society in late Victorian Britain', *Econ. Hist. Rev.*, August 1965.

6
Years of Crisis

THE PROCESSES of investment and enterprise described above
were subject to movements of expansion and contraction of
activity which lay beyond the understanding or control of those who
were involved in them. Such movements were inseparable from an
international system of exchange depending upon the unco-
ordinated decisions of a multitude of individuals, in many parts of
the world, acting in the light of hopes and fears rather than of
rational calculation. No attempt at theoretical explanation of these
movements can be made here: 'the fruit of that tree', as Professor
Ashton has observed, 'too often turns out to be the apple of discord';
but to ignore them altogether would be to lay aside an important
key to an understanding of the period, not only in its economic but
also in its social and political aspects.

Two kinds of movement have to be distinguished in considering
this question. The first and most difficult to assess in its effects is
the movement in the net barter terms of trade, i.e. the amount
which British industry had to produce for export to buy a corresponding amount, in terms of price, of food and raw materials.
Owing to cost-reducing economies, especially in textiles, the
British worker, as we have seen[1] was able to meet the relative fall in
the price of exports compared with that of imports in the post-war
period without suffering a reduction of living standards, but the
pressure on conditions of labour, especially on the length of the
working day and also on profits, was severe. From 1842, a more
favourable movement in the terms of trade developed until the

[1] See above, p. 66.

middle 1850s[1] when prices of imports once more rose somewhat faster than of exports, but again, the cost-reducing influence of technological innovation, particularly in textiles and transport by land and sea, cushioned the effects on the British worker, and living standards continued to rise. The extension of railways and steamships lowered freight charges both for exports and imports and contributed very largely to the success with which British export prices were able to keep pace with the movement of import prices in subsequent decades. It will be seen, therefore, that the threat to the favourable balance between population and productivity originating in changes in the terms of trade was met with comparative success by the continued vitality of the innovating process of British industry.

The second type of movement held a more serious menace to the stability of the nascent industrial state owing to the unpredictable and uncontrolled nature of the forces which it released. It consisted of the relatively cyclical movement of trade over an average period of about nine years' duration in which rising economic activity would reach a climax, followed by a crisis and a period of decline leading to another cycle of rise, crisis, and decline.

To some extent the problem of the trade cycle was a reflection of the random forces of nature as well as of the imperfect contrivances of men. A good harvest—essentially a reflection of appropriate weather conditions during the farmer's year—stimulated industry by increasing the demand for labour and so raising wages at the same time as the means of life became more abundant; and a bad harvest diminished the demand for labour and lowered wages while causing the price of necessities to rise. Although the effects of harvests were less directly responsible for fluctuations of investment and production than in the eighteenth century, their influence was accentuated by the corn laws, and the 'perverse fluctuations of wages', i.e. a fall in wages when prices were rising, continued to exercise their baleful effects, until the railway and the steamship finally banished the spectre of want which the failure of the home harvest had formerly raised. Superimposed upon the fluctuations of the harvest and made more violent by them were the movements of the economy dependent upon the unpredictable demands of the commodity market. With the growth of the export trade, the

[1] See Imlah, op. cit., pp. 101-2.

speculative nature of commercial production became more pronounced. Individual merchants, depending for their information
upon agents abroad, would place orders in anticipation of a hypo-
thetical demand that might or might not materialize; when existing
stocks began to run down and reports of rising prices were received
from foreign agents, the tempo of production was raised and the
'inventory cycle' began its course. All merchants, acting on similar
information, or in imitation of one another, behaved in the same
way and quickly reversed the situation which gave rise to the initial
impulse. The reversal could not be reported in time to prevent
over-production and a period of slack trade would again ensue in
order to clear away the surplus stocks. Moreover, the conditions of
the foreign markets were liable to fluctuate owing to changes in the
incomes of prospective customers as a result of harvest failure,
political instability, circumstances affecting the supply of raw
material, e.g. cotton, and perhaps especially owing to bank failures
following upon a crisis of speculation.

In view of the great distances and slow speed of transport, no
means existed of eliminating these hazards, and the early phases of
industrial growth were marked by sharp upswings of activity
bringing prosperity to producers and relatively full employment to
labour, and equally sharp reversals of fortune marked by a crop of
bankruptcies and distress of unemployed workmen. When these
adverse circumstances coincided with—and were sometimes
occasioned by—bad harvests, the conditions of large sections of the
workers became desperate and there were food riots and political
demonstrations. In the third quarter of the century, the impact of
some of these factors was minimized as a result of the growth of
transport and the increasing speed of communications. The downswings of trade were at least as sharp as before, but were less pro-
tracted until the so-called Great Depression, and the upswings
carried living standards to heights that had never been attained
before.

The trade cycle revealed itself in its complete form in 1825 when
a speculative boom outstripping those of 1791-2 and 1809-10
developed as a result of changed circumstances of the capital
market. It was new in that it was characterized by flotations of
foreign and domestic issues on an entirely unprecedented scale.
The foreign issues were mainly in the form of bonds floated by the

South American republics which were in rebellion against Spain, and in the shares of South American mining projects. The domestic issues were for railways, gas, water, insurance, mining undertakings, 'a flurry of companies' arising on a wave of confidence that was initiated by the expansion of foreign trade in 1822–3, and supported by monetary influences deriving from a change in government policy in regard to the note issue. In pursuit of its policy of returning to cash payments, the House of Commons resolved in 1819 that the Bank should pay off its small notes in gold in four years' time and that the country banks should withdraw their small notes by 1825. The Bank of England thereupon sold securities, cancelled its own small notes in 1821, and continued to buy gold to meet the situation that would arise when the country notes were withdrawn. There was an immediate outcry from currency critics led by Thomas Attwood and farmers led by Cobbett who feared that a fall in the quantity of money in circulation would cause a further disastrous fall in prices; and in deference to this criticism the Government in the Act of 1822 permitted country banks to continue to issue small notes until 1833. The Bank being left with excess reserves expanded credit both to the Government—£13 m. for military and naval pensions—and to traders—£1·5 m. to the East India Company—and from 1824 began to lend on mortgage. Between April 1823 and April 1825 the note issue of the Bank of England rose from £16·8 m. to £20·3 m.; in the same period the issues of the 500 country banks rose from £3·5 m. to £8·8 m.; and more important than either was the growth of business by the bill of exchange, cheque, and such forms of paper credit stimulated by the expansion of domestic and foreign trade. The yield on consols fell and the bank rate was reduced from 5 to 4 per cent—the first reduction for forty-nine years—and owing to the plethora of available funds, the market rate fell to 2½ per cent.

In these circumstances, economic activity rapidly assumed the characteristics of a boom. There was an immensely accelerated programme of capital goods construction, particularly cotton factories, and the biggest boom in house building on record. Stocks of raw material rose to record heights, raw cotton imports rose from 149 million lb. in 1824 to 228 million lb. in 1825; exports were stimulated by loans negotiated through Barings and Rothschilds to the mining companies in newly recognized South American states.

Hundreds of joint-stock companies sprang into existence for the promotion of railways, mining ventures, and public utilities. Speculators began to buy goods and securities on borrowed money in order to sell again, and the boom entered the stage of mania.

The turn of the tide began in October 1825 when the exchanges turned against Britain owing to the excess of imports, and gold began to leave the country; the collapse of the boom made itself felt first among the bogus schemes where profit expectations were highest, i.e. in the projects for exploiting the mineral wealth of South America; the Bank began to restrict credit and there was an internal as well as an external drain of gold; the holders of paper claims wished to realize them in hard cash and in December 1825 Sir Peter Pole, Thornton and Co., holding the accounts of forty-four country banks, closed its doors. Being unable to borrow, since the usury laws forbade the raising of interest to more than 5 per cent, merchants and manufacturers who would have been willing to pay 8 or 10 per cent for accommodation threw their accumulated stocks on the market to obtain cash at any price. The country, it was said, in the winter of 1825-6, was 'within 24 hours of barter'. The situation was saved by loans from the Bank of England to merchants on the security of goods and by the fortunate discovery by an official of the Bank of a box of small notes.

The depression which followed was especially severe in the cotton industry where the new factories had a sudden depressing effect. There were violent riots among the operatives who were said to be in unparalleled distress and whose animosity was especially directed against the newly installed power looms. The bottom of the downswing was reached quickly and recovery began to take place slowly in the following year; but there was a difficult time ahead both for workers and manufacturers. Prices continued to fall and 'an extraordinarily inflated state of demand was required in the middle twenties, thirties and forties to yield, and then only briefly, rising prices and profit margins'.[1]

The obstacles to recovery were increased by high food prices; during the years 1828-31 wheat prices were over 66s.; more than £3½ m. per annum was spent on imported wheat; they were also years of intense social unrest marked by the farm labourers' revolt of 1830, by militant trade unionism among the cotton workers and

[1] Gayer, Rostow, and Schwartz, *Growth and Fluctuation of the British Economy*, vol. i, p. 222.

the building operatives, and by the widespread demand for political reform.

Capital continued to accumulate, however, in the hands of holders of the public debt, of merchants and successful entrepreneurs both great and small, and opportunities were being sought to find lucrative outlets for idle funds. The fall in interest rates made possible another large conversion of the national debt which contributed to a lowering of the rate of interest generally and so stimulated investment. The success of Stephenson's Rocket at Rainhill and the opening of the first modern railway from Manchester to Liverpool gave a signal for a new wave of investment, and the fall in wheat prices from 58s. 8d. in 1832 to 39s. 4d. in 1835 swelled the volume of purchasing power for the products of industry and foreign trade. This factor may also have hastened the absorption of latent resources created by the investments of the 1825 boom; factories built at that time were filled with machinery and every new machine was an improvement on the last; elasticity of demand and rising population at home and abroad made it possible to realize some of the projects put forward in 1825, and the time was ripe for another general stride forward.

There was also a rise in foreign investments, especially in the U.S.A., but the main direction of new investment was at home, in railways, mines, steamships, the building industry, and above all in the cotton industry. In 1835 Dr. Kay estimated that £4 m. was being invested in cotton mills and machinery in Manchester; 58 railway bills were authorized between 1832 and 1837, 101 joint-stock banks and 21 insurance companies were formed; obsolete or luxury trades like hand-loom weaving, framework knitting, and machine-made lace found expanding markets for their products.

This last was largely a reflection of the spectacular expansion of the American market which, in 1836, accounted for a quarter of the total of British exports. They were paid for, in the main, by British funds in the form of short-term loans accepted by British export agencies on behalf of American import houses; at the same time there was a large export of British capital for the purchase of American state bonds, bank stock, railway bonds. In 1836 both Britain and America were seized by investment mania and it was fed by British speculative capital. As in 1825, the crisis first made itself felt on the margin of the economic system. In July 1836, the

American President, Andrew Jackson, issued his specie circular which ordered that payment for public lands should be made in gold, not notes. In order to protect its reserve the Bank of England raised the rate from $4\frac{1}{2}$ to 5 per cent in September 1836 and refused to discount any further American bills; importing houses cancelled orders for cotton and prices fell in America from 15 cents to 5 cents a lb.; American merchants cancelled orders in England; unemployment and rising food prices in England made 1837 a difficult year for Lancashire; but railway building kept up home demand and the rise in the bank rate brought in gold from the Continent. The currency structure appeared to be sound—so sound that the Bank sent gold in support of the tottering structure of the American banks in 1838; but in 1839 the failure of the English harvest caused the price of wheat to rise to 70s. 8d. and necessitated a large outflow of gold for the purchase of imported grain; the switch of domestic purchasing power from the products of industry to the products of agriculture was accentuated by a falling-off of exports to Belgium, Prussia, and Saxony, which were also in the throes of a commercial crisis; the financial system in America reached a state of paralysis and payments on State debts were suspended; Mississippi and Florida repudiated them altogether; and the drain of gold from the Bank led to a rise of the bank rate to 6 per cent. In spite of these conditions of financial crisis, the volume of output remained surprisingly high. Cotton manufacturers may indeed have been impelled by their high overhead costs to keep their plant running at nominal profits, or even at a loss, in the hopes of a turn of the tide, and the slow maturing investment in railways kept the iron and coal industries busy.

The wave of investments in railways, however, came to rest, and expenditure on construction work rapidly fell off; the reserves of working-class savings had been absorbed by high food prices and there was little left with which to face the emergencies of 1841-2; both these influences bore heavily on the home market and the weaker manufacturers were brought to the verge of bankruptcy; joint-stock banks, many of which were involved in the American collapse, were unable to come to their assistance, and those manufacturers who were unable to meet the crisis by further cost reductions were forced to close their doors. Manufacturers with the latest equipment were able to maintain production and some of them actually worked overtime, but there was devastation in the older centres such as Stockport where equipment was backward. Social distress was accentuated by the inadequacy and misdirection of the Poor Law, and the provocative propaganda of the Anti-Corn Law League joined with that of the Chartists to precipitate the worst social crisis of the century.

Before the year was out, there were signs of improvement; the harvest of 1842 was good, those of 1843, '44, and '45 still better. Foreign trade, assisted by the reviving confidence of the U.S.A., rapidly recovered, and by 1843 the so-called Hungry Forties were on the way to another peak of prosperity.

Whatever may be the final verdict of Sir Robert Peel's fiscal measures, there can be no doubt that his government contributed to the rise of confidence that replaced the gloom of 1842. A large conversion of debt carried out in 1843 lowered the rate of interest and released funds for more profitable enterprise; the Bank Charter Act renewed confidence in the currency; the fall of British tariffs raised expectations of profit on exports and there were reports of a disposition of merchants to buy for the foreign markets; the peace of Nanking with China opened five treaty ports to foreign trade, and the settlement of the Canadian boundary dispute with America removed a cause of international tension; the prospects of trade with Brazil were improved by the treaty of 1844. This happy coincidence of blessings induced a mood of confidence that knew no limit. At the same time 'unemployed capital abounded to an unprecedented degree', said Mr. Gladstone in 1844, 'and there could be no doubt that its investment would take a direction towards railways'. In 1844 forty-eight acts, and in 1845 120 acts, were passed authorizing railways, mainly for branch lines. There was an outflow of British capital for French and Belgian railways, and British contractors—Brassey, Mackenzie, Peto—and their highly organized gangs of British navvies began to link up continental towns with the aid of British railway iron.

As in other cases, the boom in shares came after two or three years of mounting prosperity in which the working class had participated. They had enjoyed the unusual coincidence of falling prices and a rising demand for labour. The boom—especially the boom in 'scrip'[1]—mounted to its climax in July 1845 and the signal

[1] See above, p. 38.

for recession was given when Parliament suddenly decided in July 1845 that the cash deposit for railway stock should be raised from 5 to 10 per cent. Legislative interference was the occasion, not the cause, of the collapse that followed: investment had outstripped the actual supply of investible funds. Many purchasers refused to take up their allotment of shares; those who paid in full had to limit their expenditure in other directions; income was being sacrificed to capital, and the commodity market as well as the share market declined. A further blow to the credit structure was given by the harvest failure in England, Europe, and the U.S.A., which created a world shortage of wheat and was accompanied by the utter destruction of the potato crop in Ireland. The cotton crop also fell short; the price of raw materials rose and foreign demand for manufactured products fell. In order to check speculation in cotton and wheat supplies the Bank raised discount rates from 4 per cent in January 1847 to 5½ per cent in August. But the harvest of 1847 brought down wheat prices from 105s. 2d. in May 1847 to 49s. 6d. in September, with fatal effects upon dealers in corn who had bought it at the old price. Some famous names were involved in the subsequent crash. Eleven joint-stock banks went down; bankers withdrew notes from the Bank of England and the reserve was nearing exhaustion. Would the Bank cease to issue altogether, in accordance with the terms of the Act of 1844? 'Charge what you please', said the applicants to the Bank, 'ask what you like; we do not mean to take notes; let us know that at some rate of interest we can get them and that will amply suffice.' On 25 October the Bank renewed the Chancellor's letter which allowed it to exceed the limit of issue laid down by the Act of 1844 and so enabled it to make loans on adequate security but at 8 per cent interest. Demand for liquidity fell; gold flowed in from Europe and America and the financial crisis was over.

It had been one of the sharpest and also one of the shortest on record, and essentially a domestic crisis, relatively unaffected by external influences. Politically it was insignificant; the Chartist rally was a fiasco, partly because the quartern loaf was down to 7d. but also because the mood of hopelessness had passed. Railway investment was still maturing when the crisis broke: in 1846 the length of new mileage opened was 595; in 1847 it was 780; in 1848 it was 1,191. Among the factors making for quick recovery was the unilateral adoption of free trade by Britain and the prospect which it opened of free entry of world products into the British market. At the same time, the gold discoveries in California (1848) and Australia (1851) began to play their part in the new era of prosperity that now dawned. Owing to her advanced industrial system and mercantile marine, Britain was able to supply goods to the gold-producing countries more cheaply than any other nation; in so doing, she attracted to herself the greatest proportion of the new gold supply. Being also the greatest importer of goods, the gold which flowed to Britain in payment of her goods and services rapidly flowed outwards in settlement of her own import balances. As Newmarch wrote in the last volume of the *History of Prices* in 1856, the circle of exchange was a rapidly increasing area: first the gold countries themselves; then the 'particular districts—Lancashire and Birmingham for instance—best able to meet the most urgent demand for special articles, then the districts which supplied the raw materials . . . and the area within which increased incomes are expended is necessarily wider each month'. The absorption by the U.S.A. of £50 m. of new gold helped to stimulate an immense drive westward carried forward by a burst of railway building, and a rise of imports in 1850-8 from $174 m. to $348 m. of which half came from England; British investors again began to buy American bonds and by 1860 £80 m. of American railway securities were held in Britain. Australian gold attracted a new stream of emigrants and the demand for emigrant ships stimulated a boom in shipbuilding. There was an increase of gold stocks in banks abroad—France alone absorbed £60 m. between 1848 and 1856—and an expansion of currency and credit everywhere which contributed to the business optimism of the period.

It also contributed to a rise in prices. In 1847-51 prices had fallen, but from 1852 there was a sharp upward movement which continued, except for breaks in 1857 and 1866, until 1873. The price of raw materials rose faster than of manufactures, and the terms of trade moved against Britain; but the market was strong enough to absorb these rises, and technological improvements helped to cushion the effects upon wages and profits.

A further important factor in reconciling rising costs with rising profits and wages can also be found in the effects of the wars in which Britain was engaged—especially the Crimean War and the Indian Mutiny. War expenditure, it has recently been shown, would absorb excess capacity in heavy industry, textiles, and transport, and add to employment and income without serious curtailment of non-war production. 'There would be both guns and butter.'¹ The Crimean War called for the addition of 284 steam vessels to the Fleet; 'the new iron clad steam impelled "floating batteries", with revolving turrets, put the industrial revolution on the high seas', and the iron steamships made in record time under the stress of war were available in excess of need on the return of peace. The suppression of the Indian Mutiny, leading to a boom in Indian railways and public works under the new Imperial régime, and successful war in the East, were reflected in a rise of British exports to India from £10·5 m. to £16·9 m. and to China from £2·2 m. to £5·3 m. between 1850 and 1860. The importance of this growing sector of British export trade was enhanced by its relative insulation from the main stream of fluctuations dominated by the oscillations of the American economy.

Another example of the strength which the latter exerted was already in preparation. American railways had raised funds by issue of bonds, and when they failed to pay interest on these, bond-holders foreclosed and the banks which had supported the railways failed in their turn. In October 1857 a total of 1,517 banks and 5,000 businesses in the U.S.A. collapsed; when the news reached Britain a fortnight later business houses with American connexions were faced with an immediate demand for repayment of loans and deposits. Within a month, there were numerous and disastrous bank failures. Many firms collapsed and investment was at a standstill. There was severe unemployment and acute distress and the year 1858 ranks as one of the worst for the working classes in the nineteenth century.

There was a demand for liquid resources at any cost and the Bank progressively raised the rate from 5½ to 10 per cent between July and November to protect the reserve. It had now fallen to a mere £581,000 and it was necessary to suspend the Act of 1844. The news of the Chancellor's letter did not have the calming effect that it had had ten years earlier; the internal drain continued, owing to the desperate state of the country banks, and it was necessary to exceed the statutory limit of the note issue by £2 m. which was transferred from the Issue Department to the Banking Department in exchange

¹ See J. R. T. Hughes, *Fluctuations in Trade, Industry and Finance 1850-60* (1960), p. 21.

for securities. The crisis rapidly subsided; economic activity recovered and by February 1859 the bank rate was back again at 3 per cent.

The momentum of economic advance was now being supported by the rapid industrialization of Europe and heavy British investments in India and the Colonies, and the great Victorian boom was resumed at an accelerated pace. It was interrupted by two relatively minor setbacks. In the early 1860s bad harvests combined with the Lancashire cotton famine to bring disaster to Lancashire cotton workers (though not to those employers who were fortunate enough to have large stocks of cotton and unsold goods which had accumulated from the previous years of over-production). In 1860-2 Lancashire output was halved and social distress was intense; but the troubles of Lancashire were lost in the prosperity radiated by the heavy industries under the influence of advancing railway and iron shipbuilding and the successful launching of the Bessemer steel process. Interest rates were down to 2 per cent by 1863 and investors' expectations were stimulated by the Limited Liability Act of 1862. With the end of the American Civil War, boom conditions developed in the export trade and in shipbuilding, the capital market responded by a spurt of new flotations, and the Registrar soon found his register 'cumbered with dead, stillborn or abortive companies'. 'Blind capital' was mobilized through finance companies which provided funds for public works, railways, docks, gas works, and new industrial enterprises. Many of the new companies, among them Overend Gurneys (which became a limited company in 1865) issued shares of high denomination, but called up only part. They accepted deposits at high rates of interest and used them to buy bonds and shares; 'they borrowed short and lent long', trusting to the sale of securities if need for cash arose. Half the discount business of London was in the hands of this single house, which also had interests in railways, docks, harbours in all parts of the world, and in many unsound concerns which they had taken over in payment of debts. Their debits consisted largely of deposits repayable on demand or at short notice. When, in January 1866, there was a large-scale withdrawal by banks and depositors this famous but thoroughly unsound firm found itself in difficulties, and appealed to the Bank of England for help. The Bank refused, and on 11 May —'Black Friday'—1866, Overend Gurneys failed for £5 m. There was a complete collapse of credit and the Bank had again to receive the Chancellor's letter authorizing a suspension of the Bank Charter Act and the raising of the bank rate to 10 per cent for the three following months. The follies of a single firm had precipitated a crisis that had world-wide repercussions; but it is possible that conditions in the U.S.A. were preparing for another downswing of the trade cycle and may, indeed, have helped to initiate the Overend Gurneys crisis.

The year 1867-8 was marked by unemployment and falling real wages, but the good harvest of 1869 lowered prices and stimulated domestic trade and another burst of American railway building gave a fillip to the export trade. The Franco-German war served as a brake on the incipient boom; but when the brake was removed with the coming of the peace in 1871, it broke all bounds.

Five main reasons were given by *The Economist* for the unprecedented advance that followed: the entrance of Germany, Austria-Hungary, Italy on a newer, freer, and more enterprising national career, requiring the support of the British workshop in the process of equipping them to play their part on the world stage; the phenomenal American railway boom after the Civil War; the first stages of Russian railway expansion; the shipping boom stimulated by the rise of iron and steam; the opening of the Suez Canal, and the rise in prices and wages which caused 'more expenditure and less work to take the place of frugality and diligence . . . the acquirement of riches was so easy that old virtues of diligence, skill and patience could be laid aside by masters and men'. The peak came in 1873 with an export figure of £256 m.—compared with £190 m. in 1869—'a convulsion of prosperity', in Disraeli's phrase.

In 1873 the boom broke as a result of the temporary halt in American railway building. There was a cessation of foreign lending and a glut of funds seeking investment in the home market; prices fell, especially those of the products of heavy industry but the volume of production was maintained or even rose through the application of cost-reducing techniques, and perhaps especially because of the immensely increased output of coal which had been stimulated by the expansion of the boom years. Prices would have fallen further but for the steady absorption by the Indian market of British textile and railway material; the Indian market was relatively immune from the effects of the American collapse and was sustained by a switch of British capital investments.[1] The bank rate remained at 2 per cent for long periods and ample funds were available for the reorganization of industry. The unprotected markets of Asia, Africa, and S. America as well as those of the colonial empire offered wide opportunities for British exports, and British shipping dominated the sea lanes of the world. By far the greatest victims of the price fall were the grain farmers, but meat and dairy farming continued to offer opportunities for farmers with energy and vision and the necessary resources.

There was a depression; but not of wages or of output. Alfred Marshall could see 'a depression of prices, a depression of interest, and a depression of profits'. He added, 'I cannot see any reason for believing that there is any considerable depression in any other respect.'

[1] See above, p. 81.

7
Population and the Growth of Towns

THE PARALLEL ADVANCE of industrialism and population gave
rise to a debate which still continues with vigour but still without
conclusive results. Contemporaries usually associated the growth
of population with the investment of capital and the increased
demand for labour. As Arthur Young said, in his engaging way:
'Employment is the soul of population . . . come boys, get children.
They are worth more than ever they were'; and Adam Smith
thought that with the increasing demand for labour, 'the reward of
labour must necessarily encourage in such a manner the marriage
and multiplication of labourers'. But the growth of population, by
increasing the market for goods and supplying labour for their
production, was itself a factor in stimulating capital investment, a
cause as well as a result; and the fact that a decisive upward trend in
population was in progress before the impact of industrialization
had made itself felt leaves open the question of which came first.
A provisional answer would be that a fall in the death-rate, so far
unexplained, in the middle decades of the eighteenth century,
initiated an upward movement of population both in town and
country that was sustained by economic and demographic forces
operating on the birth-rate. For the first time in urban history,
the towns began to owe their growth to a substantial excess of births
over deaths as well as to migration from an over-populated countryside.

There were many economic factors at work to raise the birth-
rate: not only investment in industry but also the expansion of agriculture to the lighter soils suitable for turnip and grain cultivation.

There was a movement of agrarian colonization to the newly enclosed areas of Derbyshire, Lincolnshire, Yorkshire with stimulating effects upon many rural industries. There was also a boom in cottage building stimulated by the growth in the size of farms and the underwriting of cottage rents by the Speenhamland system. The new industries put a premium on large families, and employers, e.g. Richard Arkwright, sometimes advertised for them.

It is, however, important to note that the rapid increase of population which resulted from the balance of births over deaths was not punished by the high death-rates which had kept population in check in earlier times, and it would appear that the scourge of epidemics which might have been expected to follow in the wake of urban overcrowding had been tamed. Leaving biological causes aside, we must attribute this largely to the environmental influence of the new economy—cotton clothes, cheap soap (since washing killed the lice which carried the infection of typhus), pottery and iron ware, houses of brick and tile, the increasing use of piped water, the work of paving and draining by improvement commissioners. The spread of improved methods of inoculation against smallpox in the villages must also be taken into account in view of recent discussions on the subject.[1] It is possible that the effect of medical knowledge and the spread of hospitals as an influence upon the death-rate has been exaggerated; but there is no doubt that there had been some improvement in the feeding of infants and in nursing, and that where vaccination was provided by the local authorities it had an immediate effect upon the child death-rate.

The study of the causes of demographic change is, however, beset with many difficulties. There were wide regional variations in the conditions governing population growth, and the sources of information upon which calculations are based, consisting mainly of parish registers of births, marriages, and deaths, were gravely deficient until after the establishment of the public registration of births in 1837. Statistical generalization regarding population growth must therefore be taken with reserve. There is, however, one important factor about which there is no doubt but which has

[1] See especially P. E. Razzell, 'Population Change in Eighteenth Century England', *Econ. Hist. Rev.*, August 1965.

been generally overlooked: the changing age structure. As Dr. Armstrong has recently shown, the population was predominantly composed of young people; and it was getting younger. In 1821 the proportion of the population falling within the age group 0–29 was 64·7 per cent; while in 1791 he has shown, by backward extrapolation, that the proportion would be of the order of 56·7 per cent; and at both dates every age group was substantially larger than the next older group.[1] There were no longer the jagged gaps arising from epidemics among the younger age groups as there had been in earlier attempts to represent the age structure, and the numbers reaching the marrying age were getting larger every generation. Need we look further for the mechanism of continuous population growth? The high birth-rate was largely a reflection of the changing age structure stemming from a fundamental shift in the death-rate dating back to the middle of the eighteenth century as a result of the weakening in the incidence of disease; and though in the towns the high birth-rate may have been a more important factor than the falling death-rate (if it fell at all), there seems no doubt that in the rural areas a substantial fall in the death-rate, side by side with the maintenance of a high birth-rate, provided a reservoir of recruitment for the towns while raising the population of the villages to a higher level than ever before. Only the surplus moved out in search of employment opportunities that the villages could not provide; the main body remained behind.

Among the factors that promoted the high birth-rate in the early years of the century the operation of the Poor Law has taken a special place. Malthus thought that the system of subsidizing wages from the poor rates stimulated early marriages in the areas where it prevailed: 'population was raised by bounties', he said, and it has recently been argued that he may have been right on the ground that the counties in which expenditure under the allowance system was especially heavy had a noticeably higher census fertility ratio (i.e. the number of children between 0 and 4 per 1,000 women between 15 and 49) than the counties that were not affected by it.[2]

[1] For further discussion of these views see W. A. Armstrong, 'La Population de l'Angleterre et du pays de Galles (1789–1815)', *Annales de Démographie Historique* (1965) (Études et Chroniques), pp. 135–89.

[2] See J. T. Krause, 'Changes in English Fertility and Mortality 1781–1850', *Econ. Hist. Review*, August 1958, p. 52.

Something of this, however, may have been due to the reduction in the number of infant deaths (including still-births) as a result of child allowances and of medical assistance provided by the parish; infants who might have died at birth and escaped registration would thus be available to swell the birth-rate; in any case, population growth in the rural areas was beginning to slow down even before the removal of allowances in 1834; and it was in the industrial districts that the natural increase of the population was especially rapid. If the fertility test is applied to the industrial population the effect of industrialism is clearly seen: for Lancashire, West Riding, Cheshire, and Staffordshire the fertility ratio in 1831 was 677; for the remainder of England it was 580, but we should remember that one of the effects of industrialism was to induce an age structure favourable to population growth, and perhaps this rather than a higher number of children per marriage accounts for the high industrial ratios. In Sussex the ratio was 716, the highest of all; but here, Professor Krause tells us, the infant death-rate was 'probably half that of the industrial counties'. Again, therefore, we must consider the possibility that the Old Poor Law operated by keeping down the infant death-rate rather than by inducing a higher birth-rate; and conversely, the decline in births noted by Professor Krause 'after the legislation of the 1830s and the 1840s' may reflect the effect of the harsher Poor Law administration upon infant mortality rather than an actual decline in the number of births per marriage.

Whatever may be the final verdict on these matters, and especially on the relative importance of birth-rates and death-rates in the first half of the nineteenth century, we can say that by 1851–2 the birth-rate was probably 35·5 and the death-rate 21·8 per thousand; by 1880–2 they had fallen slightly to 34·1 and 19·7 respectively.[1] At the same time, the age of marriage appears to have remained low: according to a Lancashire historian, the age of husbands at marriage in the cotton towns on the eve of the cotton famine was between 19 and 22 and of wives between 17 and 20; and the population boom showed no signs of losing its momentum.

Between 1801 and 1881, the population of Britain rose from 10·5 to 29·71 million and the rate of growth was maintained into the twentieth century:

[1] See D. V. Glass, *Population Policies and Movements in Europe* (1940), p. 5.

Population Increase in Britain

	1801	1811	1821	1831	1841	1851
Population (in millions)	10·5	11·97	14·09	16·26	18·53	20·81
Percentage increase		13·98	17·73	15·39	13·98	12·31

	1861	1871	1881	1891	1901
Population (in millions)	23·13	26·07	29·71	33·03	37·00
Percentage increase	11·11	12·72	13·95	11·17	12·02

Urban population grew at a phenomenal rate: between 1811 and 1821 Manchester grew by more than 40 per cent, and in the next decade by 47 per cent; between 1831 and 1841 Liverpool and Leeds each grew by more than 40 per cent and Glasgow by more than 30 per cent, in each censal period. At the same time, the rural population was also growing, though far more slowly, and in 1851 the rural districts still claimed 49·8 per cent of the total population. Under the influence of railways, the mechanization of agriculture, and the bounding prosperity of the mid-Victorian age, the balance moved rapidly in favour of the towns and by 1881 urban districts claimed 67·9 per cent of the population of England and Wales against 32·1 per cent by rural districts.

The flow of rural labour to the towns was subject to wide fluctuation owing to the influence exerted by the movement of trade. The boom of 1834–6 illustrates the flowing tide at its height and the slump of 1837–42 marks the ebb at its lowest and most desperate. The upward movement was described in a vivid report to the Poor Law Commission by Dr. Kay in 1835. The immigrants to Lancashire, he calculates, had roughly doubled in each decade between 1801 and 1831 when they reached 17,000 per annum, of whom 'few or none came from any counties south of Derbyshire or Staffordshire'. He feared the supply from this source was running low and would fail to meet the demands of the new factories equipped by steam. The growth of such towns as Stalybridge and Ashton-under-Lyne had actually brought about a decline of surrounding villages, the houses formerly occupied by hand-loom weavers being left practically deserted. Their place was likely to be taken by Irish spinners and weavers left behind as a result of the decline of their own handicraft industries, and these would willingly learn the trade of coarse calico weaving at starvation wages and move to the weaving of muslins as their skill increased. The manufacturers, however, would prefer native-born labourers from the

E

over-populated rural parishes, and he gave glowing accounts of the favourable conditions they had to offer: high wages, excellent cottages, and an especially warm welcome for parents with large families.

The scheme of sponsored migration which followed met with ill luck. In 1835-7 approximately 4,320 migrants from Suffolk and neighbouring counties were persuaded, not without difficulty, to travel by cart and canal under the supervision of the Poor Law officials to rural centres of industry in Lancashire and Cheshire. The boom collapsed in 1837; hundreds of the migrants were returned to their parishes under removal orders; many died of a smallpox epidemic, and enemies of state interference in the supply of labour could boast that their denunciation of the scheme had been justified.

But unofficial migration went on, and the episode of 1835-7 throws some light on the process by which the density of population slowly thickened in the textile centres of the north-west. It was, however, a process of attraction rather than of propulsion, and it moved with diminishing force roughly in proportion to the distance between the centre of attraction—the high-wage areas—and the source of supply. Thus in 1851, of every 10,000 people in Lancashire, 408 were born in Cheshire, 81 in Derbyshire, 45 in Shropshire, 10 in Leicestershire, 6 in Northants., 3 in Hertfordshire, and 2 in Bedfordshire. Of every 10,000 in London, 103 were from Hertfordshire, 33 from Bedfordshire, 45 from Northants., 25 from Leicestershire, and 20 from Derbyshire, besides a very large number from the immediately surrounding counties. But the movement was not by any means a steady one; Dr. Kay's average of 17,000 per annum into Lancashire in the decade 1821-31 was compatible with wide fluctuations, and in the years of depression, such as those of 1837-43, there was a substantial backward flow. The census of 1841 reveals a thinning of population in many factory towns through stoppage of factories; one house in every five in Stockport was empty; Oldham had 1,800 empty houses and some housed several families: between 1841 and 1843 more than 15,000 persons were removed under the settlement laws from various industrial towns in Lancashire, Yorkshire, and Cheshire; of these 12,000 have been traced to their places of settlement; 7,000 to Lancashire, the West Riding, and Cheshire; over 4,600 to Ireland, the rest in dwindling numbers as the radius lengthens. When the wheels of industry began to whirr to another high speed record in 1845 the centripetal movement of fluid labour began again and was not checked on an equal scale until the cotton famine in the American Civil War.

Whether the pattern of recruitment of the textile centres was repeated in the centres of heavy industry is by no means certain. Coal mining was rarely carried on in large towns; it was more usually found in isolated communities, often in rural surroundings and was self-contained in social habits and traditional skill. There is evidence of some, but not of strong, influx from outside. 'Pitmen must be bred to their work', the Poor Law Commission was told in 1834, 'the numbers cannot be recruited from any other source.' There were, however, some reinforcements from the lead mines of Derbyshire, and the over-populated villages of west Wales were relieved of their surplus when the railways linked them with the heavy industries after 1850.

In the iron industry labour was more mobile and responsive to the ebb and flow of demand and also to the stimulus of fiercely competitive employers. Scottish employers attracted English labour 'by offering good houses, gardens and high wages', while Staffordshire employers recruited men from Scotland and Wales. Agents who were sent out among Welsh agricultural workers sometimes had to overcome a barrier of prejudice created by the reputation for drunkenness and profligacy of the iron workers, but the pressure of population and the influence of the railways combined to break it down. In the peak periods of production, employers accused one another of enticement of skilled workers; in slack times they tried to keep their skilled labour together by finding alternative forms of work, and they complained of the loss through emigration to the U.S.A. and European iron centres.

The speed at which the great urban and industrial centres grew did not create, it drew attention to, the conditions of squalor and overcrowding in which the labouring class had always lived. The shockingly bad housing and the appallingly high death-rate of the urban poor were permanent features of town life, and indifference born of familiarity was the greatest obstacle to the formulation of a new attitude to meet the sudden inflation of an old evil. The work of improvement commissioners in paving, lighting, and water supply was overwhelmed by the tide of new building, and the new towns grew up in blind response to current need. Buildings were frequently erected back-to-back along narrow alleys or around courts which may once have been gardens and were now closed in on all four sides and entered by a tunnel. They often grew too fast to be connected with the existing 'low pressure' water supplies and had to rely upon water carriers, selling water by the pail, until local engineers began to pump water by steam engine from the rivers to reservoirs where it was filtered and supplied under pressure to a stand pipe in the streets and courts. This essential service, begun in Nottingham by a young engineer, Thomas Hawkesley in 1829, spread rapidly to most towns of substantial size, and must be taken into account among the factors that prevented the return of pre-industrial urban death-rates.

That such a possibility hovered over the towns of Victorian England cannot be ignored; for the country as a whole, the death-rate seems to have fallen between 1820 and 1840, but for some large towns there is reason to think that it was rising. Glasgow, Manchester, and Liverpool had some notoriously black spots, but so also had the Yorkshire woollen towns, and half the families in Newcastle, where the indifference by the local authorities amounted to criminal neglect, lived in or shared one single room when it was struck by the full force of the cholera epidemic of 1853. Cholera must be accounted one of the beneficent influences of the nineteenth century: it struck terror as though it had been the bubonic plague but was incomparably less destructive of life; and, though the secret of its origin was hidden from scientists and administrators alike until the time of Pasteur, it stimulated a campaign which struck at the roots of the far more deadly forms of disease which were associated with overcrowding. Witnesses to the inquiries of the 1840s never wearied of drawing attention to the wide disparity in the chances of life in different parts of the country and in different areas of the same town, but high death-rates were usually accompanied by inordinately high birth-rates and the direct checks of disease failed of their effect where the conditions for their operation were most favourable.

One of the reasons for the congestion was that employment was so often of a casual nature and that the workers had always to be on the spot in order to take the opportunity of earning when it arose.

It was—as it always had been—necessary for the women and girls of the family to contribute to the family income, and the family group had to live within walking distance of their different places of employment. The market for casual labour was a factor in determining the density of population; and the increasing activity of the economy called for a rising supply of casual labour.[1] Lord Shaftesbury in 1884 pointed out that though there had been improvement in the sanitary conditions of the poor of London, the problem of overcrowding had become not less but more serious with the passage of time.

Another reason, and perhaps the most important, was to be found in the financial factors which governed the housing of the working classes. The houses were built as a speculation in competition with other forms of investment and therefore generally attracted small-scale capitalists who were in a position to effect economies by direct oversight of all the stages of building, and so were able to supply the demand at a price which the customer could pay. The price charged by the ground landlord, sometimes reaching fantastic heights, and the taxation on bricks and timber amounting, according to a statement of Joseph Hume in 1850, to no less than £20 on a cottage which cost £60, were irreducible charges on the capital outlay, and the only economies which could be made were at the expense of the consumer. So-called 'jerry building' was inevitable, and the 'jerry builder' was an indispensable agent in the nation-wide operation of housing the working classes.

Some of the early factory communities—Cromford, Belper, Styal—were extremely well housed, and it might be found that, where factory masters undertook the housing of their work-people, conditions were well above the average, at least in the industrial village communities. Edmund Ashworth claimed in 1840 that for twenty years he had made every successive series of cottages more expensive and more convenient than the last, and the domestic amenities which he could offer—two rooms down and two rooms up, sometimes three, with oven and boiler and a good kitchen grate—were held out as an attraction to the unemployed labourers of the eastern counties in 1835. There were a few deliberately planned industrial communities, notably that of Robert Owen at New

[1] See W. Ashworth, *Genesis of British Town Planning* (1954), on which this section is largely based.

Lanark, the village of Battersea, built to house the workers of Prices' candle factory in 1853, and above all the model town of Saltaire built in 1851 by the self-made woollen manufacturer, Titus Salt of Bradford, in which attention was paid not only to health and accommodation but also to amenities such as a library institute, concert and lecture hall, and a public park. It was acclaimed as a model but not followed as an example, and the industrial communities which sprang up round the iron works of South Wales, the collieries of the Midlands, and the railway shops of Crewe and Swindon were monotonous and dreary, though they were free from the worst evils of the 'self-generated industrial agglomerations' that sprang up round the centres of the older industrial towns.

Gradually, through the tireless energies of individuals and philanthropic organizations, a new conception of urban life made itself felt, and the struggle for a minimum of provision for the industrial population called forth the highest as well as some of the most sordidly calculating attributes of the age. The campaign for public health called not only for idealism but for heroic courage and persistence. In his Report of 1839 Southwood Smith informed the Poor Law Commissioners that both relieving officers and medical men had lost their lives in consequence of the brief stay which they had to make in certain parts of East London in the performance of their duties. Edwin Chadwick involved himself in continuous controversy with doctors and engineers in his life-long effort to sell the 'sanitary idea' to the local authorities; the mass production of iron and earthenware piping provided the necessary equipment, but until biological science came to the aid of technology through the work of Louis Pasteur, it was still possible for a man of Chadwick's stature to confound the symptom with the cause. 'No filth in the sewers—all in the rivers' was *The Times*'s summary of his prescription for the cholera outbreaks of 1848-9 and 1852-3; he cleared the air but poisoned the water, with frightful effects upon mortality and unfortunate consequences to the reputation of the Board of Health.

The Public Health Act of 1848 appointed a General Board of Health which could establish local boards at the request of the inhabitants or where the death-rate reached a prescribed figure, but in 1854-8 the Board was allowed to lapse and its powers were taken over by the Privy Council and the Home Office acting through their medical officer, John Simon. But the work started by the great pioneers of the 1830s went on in the towns themselves, and the massive indifference which they encountered from the middle classes was gradually eroded away by appeals to self-interest through calculation of the economic benefits to be derived from better standards of national health. The possibility of effecting a social revolution through the instrument of democratic municipal government slowly took shape in response partly to the public spirit of dedicated local leaders, but also to the realization on the part of voters enfranchised by the Municipal Corporations Act of 1835 of the solid economic stakes involved. The loss of earnings of labour as a result of sickness, the cost of restraining the poor from crime as a result of overcrowding and promiscuity, the relief which would accrue to poor rates from improved health, were the stock arguments advanced by organizations for the improvement of the industrious classes, and by propagandist bodies such as the Health of Towns Association. Doctors, lawyers, ministers of religion, engineers, traders, and industrialists in every large town took upon themselves the repugnant and dangerous task of finding out the facts and devising remedies for this, the greatest social problem of the age.

An important practical contribution was made by philanthropic bodies which tried to ensure certain minimum standards of housing, while keeping rents below the level which the market permitted. The Metropolitan Association for Improving the Dwellings of the Industrious Classes and the Society for the Improvement of the Conditions of the Labouring Classes founded in 1844, the Improved Industrial Dwellings Co., the Peabody Trust and others opened model blocks of dwellings and were able to show a satisfactory return upon the investment. But the rents charged took them out of the reach of those whose need was greatest and Octavia Hill pointed out in 1875 that all the private benevolence in London over the previous thirty years had housed only 26,000 people, equivalent to a little more than the increase in London population every six months. Whereas a large part of the population earned less than £1 a week, the tenants of the housing societies were found to earn from 23s. to 28s. a week. It was admitted by one of them that the problem of housing the very poor on commercial principles was insoluble because the expense of repairs rose to 50 per cent of the rental, whereas the normal proportion was 12 per cent, and the difficulty of collecting rents increased with the poverty of the tenants.

Steps were also being taken to impose standards on new building through local enactments which included provisions enforcing minimum standards of accommodation, sanitation, and water supply; some towns appointed committees and officers to carry out improvements before the passing of the Health Act of 1848; but both before and after its passing they could proceed only by persuasion and example, not by compulsion. They were able to secure the co-operation of owners in the opening of closed courts and the cleansing of walls by lime-washing, introducing water supply under pressure, paving and draining, and they began to make an attack on the problem of sewage disposal by large-scale engineering works or in other ways.

After the lapse of the Public Health Board in 1858 central direction virtually came to an end, but in 1866 and 1871 Acts were passed which made sanitary inspection obligatory on local authorities and overcrowding a nuisance. They also empowered the Secretary of State, upon complaints received, to compel authorities to remove nuisances and to provide sewers and water supplies, and the Act of 1875 made it possible for local authorities to order the demolition and reconstruction of whole sections of a town.

Where local acts were applied, a comparison of urban building before and after 1850 shows that the public health campaign was not without effect. Large-scale clearance schemes were undertaken in a number of overcrowded centres, but the mere removal of a black spot created more congestion in the peripheral areas owing to the failure of local authorities to provide alternative accommodation. The railway termini of great cities similarly contributed to the squalor by clearing away densely populated areas without effectively providing for the unfortunate inhabitants. While the standard of building improved and the provision of municipal services made rapid strides, the problems of overcrowding remained insoluble in the absence of a publicly supported housing programme.

Local authorities were by no means blind to the needs of the times. They sometimes experimented in housing the working classes under Lord Shaftesbury's Act of 1851, but as with the private bodies, they found themselves facing the problem of reconciling the cost of building and maintenance with the wage level of those who were in most need of housing accommodation, and public opinion, including the opinion of Octavia Hill, was hostile. Octavia Hill told the Royal Commission of 1884–5 that Shaftesbury's Act was no longer necessary as the public mind was awakened to the problem, and local authorities persistently denied the need to supplement the efforts of private enterprise. In Birmingham, however, where slum clearance was on a scale that dwarfed the efforts of any town outside London, the bankruptcy of this negative policy was made inescapably plain by Joseph Chamberlain, who, in his evidence to the same Commission, said:

We indulged in Birmingham in this tremendous luxury of an improvement scheme to reconstruct a single district of the town at the cost of half a million of money; but we have exhausted all our capacities in that respect; we cannot undertake to burden the ratepayers any more for that purpose; and unless any means can be found by which similar schemes can be carried out at much less cost, we have done all that this generation at any rate will be able to do, I should say.[1]

Judged by the standards of a later age, the achievements of the Victorians in meeting the social problems of population growth were lamentably inadequate; but there were some grounds for the relative complacency with which leaders of opinion regarded the rate of progress. Lord Shaftesbury on his eighty-third birthday in 1884 remarked on 'the enormous improvement' in the housing and sanitation of London during the previous thirty years, and it may well be true that London was the healthiest large town in the world. The death-rate continued to fall, though more slowly: the London death-rate fell from 23·8 per thousand in 1841–51 to 21 per thousand in 1871–81. In the industrial towns of the north in which the problems of overcrowding were even worse than in London, there was a fall from 28·1 to 24·6; in residential towns both in the north and south the rate had fallen to 20 or slightly below; in the colliery districts it fell only slightly from 23·4 to 23·1. Since the birth-rate still remained high, the excess of births over deaths tended to widen; for the country as a whole it was 14 per thousand, which accounted for an increase of over 300,000 per annum by the 1880s; and of this annual increase, the greatest contribution was made by the industrial

---

[1] Royal Commission on Housing 1884–5, q. 12,403. I owe the reference to the kindness of Prof. T. C. Barker.

areas where the excess of births reached 18·8 per thousand in the northern colliery districts and 16·1 per thousand in the northern textile towns. The northern towns, it has been said, triumphed over the south less by attracting migrants than by superior fertility: a birth-rate of 38·7 to 41·9 in 1871–81 compared to 34·7 in London, 29·4 in the southern residential towns, and 31·3 in the southern rural areas.

The annual increment of population, great as it was, would have been substantially larger if it had not been for emigration. In the years 1815–30 the outflow of roughly 25,000 a year from the United Kingdom had been predominantly of Irish and Scottish origin and, as far as Great Britain was concerned, was more than counterbalanced by an intake of Irish immigrants. The troubled years of 1830–2 took the total of emigrants to 100,000, a peak not surpassed until 1842, when it reached 130,000, and again in the crisis years 1847–9 when it reached an average of over 250,000. From this point the proportion of Irish sank and a substantial majority of the 2,466,000 who left for foreign shores between 1853 and 1880 were British. The second phase of emigration differs from the first by showing some degree of responsiveness to economic prosperity and the export of capital. The boom in capital exports in 1870–3 coincided with a peak in emigration, and when export of capital started again in the 1880s and real wages made their record advance, emigration rose to a slightly higher peak. Moreover, the countries which borrowed most secured the most immigrants. This movement tended to accentuate the cyclical effects on wages and on house rents, causing an upward pressure on wages through increased shortage of labour and a downward movement of house rents through lowered demand for houses during an upswing and the reverse effect during the downswing.

The change in the character of migration had another and more welcome consequence on the housing of the working classes. The influx of Irish in the first half of the century added a touch of the macabre to an already desperate situation in the towns where they congregated. In 1834–5 there may have been 150,000 Irish in Lancashire, and one-fifth of the population of Manchester and one-sixth of Glasgow were thought to be Irish. There was also a large concentration in Middlesex and Surrey, a total of settled and unsettled of 451,000 in 1841. In the terrible year of 1846 another

quarter of a million arrived, and in spite of a large efflux to the
U.S.A. the total in England in 1851 was 727,000—a figure from
which it rapidly declined. The Irish were moved about the country
largely at the expense of English ratepayers under the vagrancy
laws, a conveyance by coach from London to Liverpool being provided at a cost of £4. 11s. 8d., and a ticket to Ireland for a roughly
similar amount. After a couple or more seasons in England they
might expect to save enough for departure for America, where they
arrived with an average capital of £15 per head after having paid
£5 passage money. 'On one ship, the *Ocean Monarch*,' it was
reported in 1849 that '320 immigrants had £10,000, an average of
over £30 per person.' Remittance back to the United Kingdom
may have reduced the net outflow to £12 per head in 1847 and £10
thereafter. The Irish were able to accumulate these substantial
sums by hard work at any kind of labour that offered itself, and
harder living conditions than only the most hopeless of English
labourers would tolerate, in particular the cellar dwellings of
Manchester and Liverpool and the terrible 'wynds' of Glasgow.
They provided strike leaders and strike breakers, but by their contribution to the advance of cotton, iron, coal, transport, and agriculture, they helped to raise the rate of total industrial production
for the period 1815-47 to the highest of the century.

8

Labour in the 'Industry State'

THE WELL-BEING OF LABOUR during the transition to industrialism depended, in the last resort, on the changing ratio of production to the growth of population, and there were numerous occasions in the first half of the century when the outcome of this race did not appear to favour the cause of labour. This was especially the case in the years after 1815, and the resultant social pressures were probably the most severe of the century. Even when these were relieved after the upswing of the early 1820s, a permanent problem of rural under-employment remained, and the subsequent downswings of the trade cycle caused mass unemployment among industrial workers, especially in the non-mechanized branches of industry. This chronic condition of labour surplus had the paradoxical result of slowing down the rate of mechanization and at the same time of inducing a willingness on the part of entrepreneurs to take risks; the rugged individualism with which the age is generally credited was to some extent a reflection of the low price at which labour for risky enterprises could be bought.[1]

Owing to the over-abundant labour supply and also to the weakness of trade-union organization, it was inevitable that a disproportionately small share of the rising national product should go to labour; and the proportion would have been smaller still if the progress of agricultural innovation had not removed the danger of rising prices and a consequent pressure on wages and a curtailment of investment. The more skilled section of the workers, at

[1] See H. J. Habakkuk, *American and British Technology in the 19th Century*, Ch. V, and J. R. T. Hughes, *Fluctuations in Trade and Finance 1850-1860*, pp. 288-9.

least those who could deploy their skill in the mechanized branches of industry, undoubtedly made substantial gains; but the great majority could not hope to rise above a low subsistence standard, and even this was snatched from many of them in the course of the fluctuations to which the economic system was only too liable. It is easy to charge governments with callous neglect and to say that something should have been done to relieve distress; as we shall see, some very important things (though not always the right ones) were done, but within the tripartite limitations of population pressure, commercial fluctuations, and an exaggerated fear regarding the diminishing supply of available land, governments had only a restricted field for manœuvre on the social front; and when conditions improved in the second half of the century, the course that had been set in the harsh days of *laissez-faire* had become a fixed habit of mind, and it required the advance of industrial democracy and an intellectual revolution to change it.

Those who, at the beginning of the century, had the responsibility for setting the course found themselves at the parting of the ways. On the one side was the paternalistic tradition of action through the local justices in the spirit of the Elizabethan poor law; on the other the theory of freedom from state interference embodied in the doctrine of the harmony of interests developed by Adam Smith, according to which each individual, if left to pursue his own interests, would be led as 'by an invisible hand', to advance the interests of all.

The proposals of the traditionalist school of thought took the form of Bills for the fixing of minimum wages, for various forms of provision of allotments for agricultural labourers, and for erecting a rudimentary structure of national insurance for sickness and old age on the basis of the existing friendly societies. The machinery for minimum wage regulation disappeared in 1813 with the repeal of the wages clauses of the Act of 1563, but the campaign for supplementing wages through allotment schemes fluttered into life whenever rural unrest reached danger point—in 1795 and 1796 when both Sir John Sinclair and the Prime Minister, Pitt, introduced proposals of this kind; in 1816-19 and in 1831-2 when agrarian disorders had drawn attention to the agricultural labourers' distress. Such schemes had to meet not only the inertia and indifference of the landed interest but also the theoretical opposition of those who believed, with Malthus (whose *Essay on Population* first appeared in 1798) that they would lead to an increase of population and to still greater rural poverty. Acts were passed to enable parishes to inaugurate allotment schemes but farmers were loth to release land for this purpose, and private provision by benevolent landlords and eminent churchmen, highly successful though some of them were, touched only the fringe of the problem. A garden and a pig were as much as most labourers could hope for, and not all were successful in attaining even this modest supplement to their meagre wages.

The development of friendly societies into a national provision of insurance has a history going back to the Revd. T. Acland's scheme of 1786, and was recommended by Jeremy Bentham in an unpublished pamphlet in 1794. It continued to have its advocates, especially J. C. Curwen, a noted landlord and colliery owner who inaugurated an extensive scheme among his own employees at Workington and pressed it upon Parliament as a working model for general adoption. He would have united the Malthusian proposal for the abolition of the poor laws with a national system of insurance against sickness and old age, and accident benefits for dependants, based on joint subscription by workers, employers, and the parish. The Revd. J. T. Becher, a Nottinghamshire magistrate, drew the attention of the Poor Law Commission in 1833 to the constructive possibilities which he had himself experienced in the co-operation of poor law authorities and friendly societies, but without effect. Though the members of the Commission approved of self-help in principle, they were too closely wedded to the policy of deterrence to give it overt encouragement by any form of public support.

The landed classes, who largely monopolized political power, regarded the existing poor law structure as a social heritage which, with all its faults, reflected the essentially paternalistic character of social relations. They could not be expected to welcome proposals that appeared to involve a surrender of local authority to new and more centralized agencies of the State; but the growth of dependent poverty appeared to be a social and economic menace; and it was inevitable, in the circumstances of the time, that the more deterrent aspects of contemporary social thought, particularly the ideas of Bentham and Malthus, should prevail. They were the ideas of individualism, i.e. that each man should be responsible for his own and his family's maintenance by his own labour; the labourer, for the sake of his manhood as well as for the welfare of the State, should stand on his own feet. But ideas of individualism did not necessarily imply opposition to all forms of State interference. On the contrary, Bentham might be described as a precursor of the Fabians in his advocacy of State action to promote the greatest happiness of the greatest number—the principle of utility. For this supreme end he proposed, in effect, a revolution in the machinery of administration in order to achieve a universal minimum of justice, health, and education; and when he found that the existing ruling class were primarily interested in promoting the happiness, not of the greatest number, but of themselves, he became an advocate of a radical widening of the franchise.

If Benthamite thought had its collectivist side,[1] the thought of Malthus had its paternalistic side. He differed from his fellow economists in recognizing the danger of general unemployment, and his whole purpose in making population the centre of social policy was to show that the solution of the problem of poverty lay in the power of the labouring classes to limit their own numbers through restraint of marriage, a restraint that the State could assist by promoting schemes of education. Like Bentham, he was substituting the ideal man with the knowledge and strength of character to shape his own life for the actual man of the overcrowded towns and villages, subject to the ebb and flow of the demand for labour, and relying on the poor law and private charity to meet emergencies.

Mention should also be made of another important influence, and perhaps the most pervasive of all, that of the dissenting chapels, under the growing influence of the evangelical revival. They greatly strengthened the cause of individualism through the emphasis they placed on the relation that they believed to exist between a man's physical well-being and his moral condition: success in life was the result of hard work and self-denial, and neither State help nor private charity could be made a substitute for a man's own efforts. Their doctrine was the religious counterpart of the theory of the economists who said that since the economy

---

[1] Cf. unpublished evidence of Edwin Chadwick on 'Collateral Aids' for the Poor Law Report of 1834 in which he spoke of finding money for housing in order to improve public health: of parks, zoos, museums, theatres as an antidote to drunkenness; and of advancing education in order to check crime and poverty. See S. E. Finer, *Edwin Chadwick*, p. 70.

was self-regulating, and since the supply of one set of commodities automatically constituted the demand for another, there could be no such thing as 'general gluts' or long-term unemployment: so long as there was maximum freedom of capital and labour to move to their alternative uses, the processes of capital accumulation and investment would prevent unemployment from being more than a transient phenomenon. But there was one further condition—the will to work; and the chapels gave it the added strength of a moral sanction, the passport to spiritual regeneration as well as to worldly success. By so doing, they helped to classify 'the poor' as a separate part of the nation for whom nothing directly could be done since the solution of their difficulties lay, in the last resort, in their own hands; and the housing conditions under which they lived contributed to this crystallization of the 'two nations' by producing a population 'from which', as one of the most devoted social workers in one of the worst towns in England said, 'the heart turns in disgust which almost overpowers the feeling of commiseration'. The sheer growth of numbers, reinforced in many industrial centres by Irish workers for whom a house was merely a shelter from the elements, presented a problem before which the stoutest heart might quail; but it is important to remember that in every town, even in the areas most afflicted by these evils, there were always dedicated individuals who felt impelled to spend their lives in the service of their most wretched fellow townsmen, even if they had nothing to offer them but spiritual regeneration through hard work and self-denial.

At the same time, the advance of 'vital religion' among Anglican circles infused new energy into traditional paternalism, as was seen in the work of Tory evangelicals such as Lord Shaftesbury, Michael Sadler, Richard Oastler; and the title of one of Oastler's pamphlets —*The Huddersfield Dissenters stark staring mad!!! The fourth letter to Edward Baines Esq., M.P.*—shows the depth of feeling between them and their rival religionists over the matter of State interference in regard to factory children. The Tory evangelicals were not alone in their campaign against what they believed to be the heartless individualism of Benthamite radicals and dissenting champions of *laissez-faire*, many of whom, like Edward Baines, were successful manufacturers. They could draw upon the resentment which the landed classes felt for the rising class of industrial capitalists who challenged their monopoly of political power and undermined their economic security by attacks on the Corn Laws. The landed classes were glad to use the agitation on the subject of the factory children as a base for a counter attack upon the soulless materialism of industrial capitalism and 'the economics of calculation'. Thus it came about that the adaptation of social policy in Britain to the economic changes of machine industry and the free market was largely achieved by an alliance of forces between Benthamite interventionists, under the leadership of Edwin Chadwick, and the forces of traditional paternalism under the leadership of Lord Shaftesbury.

The part played by the economists in the controversy has sometimes been misunderstood. It is true that their attention was focused on the processes of capital accumulation which were obviously vital in an age of rapid and simultaneous advance in so many directions; and since, in their opinion, the only lasting remedy for social ills rested with the labouring classes themselves through the limitation of their own numbers, there was nothing the State could do *directly* to assist them; but there was much that could be done *indirectly*, first by assisting the efficient functioning of the economic process through legislation affecting banking, commercial policy, and the capital market, and secondly through social legislation, such as education and public health, which would help the wage-earning classes to help themselves. They were also prepared to interfere directly for the protection of those who were unable to protect themselves, e.g. the factory children. 'No facts have been proved to me', said McCulloch, 'which show that it is proper to keep a child of eleven years old for twelve hours a day in attendance on the employment, however light, of a factory . . . it is absurd to contend that children have the power to judge for themselves in such matters.' This seems a tepid reaction to the crying scandal of child labour in factories, but it is at least more constructive than that of trade unionists and the parents themselves who thought that children should work alongside adults in the factory as they did in the family workshops, e.g. for a ten-hour working day even when the State had fixed it (by the Act of 1833) at nine.[1]

The regulation of factory labour was the first of the new problems arising from the growth of machine industry with which the State

[1] But a forty-eight-hour week.

attempted to deal. Until the Benthamites seized the initiative in the reformed House of Commons and inaugurated the Royal Commission of Enquiry—a specifically Benthamite device—which led to the Act of 1833, the record is one of continuously frustrated effort. The earlier Acts—1802, 1819, 1820, 1825, 1829, 1831—at least bore witness to a persistent effort of reform. They also achieved the recognition of the important principle of State regulation of child labour, whether that of children sent to the factory by their parents or of pauper children sent by parishes; and the inauguration of machinery for the collection of information in the form of time books kept by employers which were liable to inspection by J.P.s was a definite advance. The Act of 1833 was in a different category and introduced the Benthamite principles of a paid inspectorate producing annual reports to the Home Office, the nine-hour day and compulsory education for children between 9 and 13, and the twelve-hour day for young persons between 13 and 18, to all but silk factories. It involved a reorganization of the labour force within the factory on the basis of having relays of children to work with the adults whose labour was not regulated; it also involved a very considerable burden of book-keeping and (for those manufacturers who performed their duties conscientiously) considerable expense in order to comply with the education clauses. Only the very large and very public-spirited factory masters could be expected to give it a fair trial, and it was as one of these that R. H. Greg spoke in 1837. 'Meanwhile', he wrote, 'since you must educate your children, do it well; your duty as Christians, your comfort as citizens, your interest as mill owners, your credit as men of sense, suggest that the intention of the legislature in this point should be carried into full execution,' and he added, with the emphasis of block capitals, 'we know but ONE remedy for the evils of the "Factory System" . . . we mean EDUCATION', i.e. a State system of compulsory education for all.

So radical a measure as the 1833 Factory Act could not have been passed by the arguments of the Benthamites alone: it had behind it the support of the landed interest who welcomed the opportunity which the factory question offered to abuse and humiliate the factory owners, the representatives of the new capitalist class that was rising to supplant them. The campaign against them, led by Sadler, was 'emphatically partisan', as Engels said, and involved the 'most distorted and erroneous statements', but it served the purpose of strengthening the government's resolution when the volume of opposition against the Act threatened to bring about its repeal. The government, goaded by Lord Shaftesbury (Sadler's successor), had no option but to enforce it, and indeed to strengthen it, and in the teeth of opposition from men, masters, and parents of children, the first instalment of Benthamite collectivism was built into the administrative structure of the industrial State.

The same forces of Benthamite radicalism and evangelical Toryism were mobilized under the same leadership to pass the Mines Act of 1842 and the Factory Act of 1844. The former is important as marking the appointment of the first inspector of labour connected with coal mines (though he was not expected to go underground); it is also noteworthy for the choice of the official to fill this post: H. S. Tremenheere, who is reported to have been responsible for the promotion of fourteen Acts of Parliament, all of them interventionist and improving, ranging from underground mines inspection to bakehouse regulation. He is an example of the devoted civil servants, of whom Leonard Horner, the factory inspector, is another, who carried forward the growing responsibilities of the State in the light of their consciences rather than of abstract theory. 'Utilitarianism', Tremenheere wrote to Harriet Martineau,

or whatever doctrine it was that taught employers to think that all they had to do was to pay their people wages and that self-interest of the latter would lead them to take care of themselves, is responsible for much of the formidable demoralization and disaffection of large masses of the lower classes . . . it will require the unremitting exertions of the powers and authorities, intellectual and social (under the guidance of the Christian faith), of the upper order of society, to prevent the lower from retrograding in civilization and bringing down the rest with them.

The Factory Act of 1844 did not concede the ten-hour principle for adult workers, but in the debate upon it there was general recognition that a new stage had now been reached and that factory regulation was no longer confined simply to humanitarian measures to meet cases of extreme hardship; and in 1847—a year of crisis and widespread unemployment—the ten-hour day was formally conceded to women and young persons and made fully effective in 1850 when the evils of the relay system were finally removed. An

Act was also passed in 1844 to provide for greater safety and better service on railways, and even for the purchase of railways by the State, if necessary, though the necessity was never deemed to arise. The Tory Parliament of 1841 was induced by the appalling revelations of three doctors, Southwood Smith, Arnott, and Kay-Shuttleworth, and also by the patent miseries of the town populations as shown by the Chartist agitation, to initiate the famous inquiries into public health under the leadership of the greatest of all civil servants, Edwin Chadwick, who had 10,000 copies of his famous Report of 1842 circulated free of charge and started the course of events which moved steadily to the first Public Health Act of 1848.

This achievement represented the climax of the period of Benthamite collectivism; the impetus which had carried it forward began to wane in the atmosphere of Victorian prosperity and in face of the hostilities it had aroused. Master John Bull, it was said by *The Times*, would not be soaped and scrubbed by Mr. Chadwick; and the General Board of Health was allowed to lapse. Moreover, the influence of the more doctrinaire wing of *laissez-faire*, after the spectacular victory of the extreme free-traders over the landlords in regard to the Corn Laws, was now in the ascendant. Its chief voice was that of John Bright, who boasted that he had opposed every enactment for the regulation of labour in factory or mine, every measure for the promotion of public health or for the abatement of the smoke nuisance in large towns, and even the restriction of the licensing laws. He himself was a model employer, a virulent hater of landlords, and a radical democrat in favour of manhood suffrage, but he regarded State interference as unnecessary and as an intolerable invasion of the private domain of the citizen. A religious zealot of another school, Lord Shaftesbury, however, succeeded in obtaining the commission on child labour in 1861 which revealed, among other things, the continued scandal of excessively long hours in the unregulated factories and workshops, and the unbelievable barbarities that were still being practised by master chimney sweeps on climbing-boys in large towns. By a succession of Acts culminating in the comprehensive Act of 1878, State regulation was extended to all 'factories' employing fifty or more workers (with some minor exceptions) and to 'workshops' employing less than fifty employees; and the Education Acts of 1870, 1873, and

1876 placed the factory code on the firm foundation of compulsory education for children under thirteen.

The Mines Act of 1842, which had forbidden the underground employment of females (in which it had been anticipated by the collective action of the men themselves in the northern pits) and of boys under the age of ten, was followed by the Acts of 1855 and 1856 which introduced minimum standards of safety under penalties; but it was not until 1872 that the persistent obstruction by mine owners who were also J.P.s was effectively removed by the Act which made it unlawful for any owner or manager to adjudicate on any offence under the mining code. The work of mines inspectors, especially Thomas Evans and Herbert Macksworth, who had fought a twenty years' battle for safety in the fiery mines of South Wales, was beginning to yield results.

The civil servants were quietly at work in other areas of activity. Dr. Kay-Shuttleworth, who from 1839 was secretary to the Privy Council Committee on Education, was able to lay down regulations for training teachers and to make unobtrusive preparations for the Education Act of 1870 without arousing the animosities of the religious bodies which had killed the hopes of government proposals for a national system of education in 1843. Similarly John Simon was able to make important progress in public health by promoting the Local Government Act of 1858 which enabled local authorities to undertake paving and draining. Further Acts followed—in 1866 the Torrens Act and 1875 the Cross Act—which together authorized slum clearance, and it could no longer be said that the inviolability of property rights presented an insuperable obstacle to effective health reform or town planning.

Under the combined influence of Benthamite collectivism and evangelical Toryism, the campaigns for an effective code of labour regulations, public health, and education made significant progress. In regard to the poor law, however, the problem was felt to be too serious to admit of any compromise with the claims of humanitarianism. The agricultural labourers were absorbing nearly £3 m. out of £6·8 m. raised for poor relief, and paternalism took the form of deterrence for the labourers' own good. The Act of 1834, carried out under the Benthamite rubric of inquiry and centralized direction, was based upon the abstract proposition that 'Every penny bestowed that tends to render the condition of the pauper more eligible than that of the independent labourer is a bounty on indolence and vice'; and the instrument for its application was the workhouse test, with its corollary, the less eligibility principle, i.e. strict workhouse conditions which would be less attractive than any alternative form of labour. Parishes were to be formed into Unions under Poor Law Guardians consisting of J.P.s and members elected by ratepayers; and three Poor Law Commissioners were appointed with power to make—but not necessarily to enforce —recommendations for the carrying out of a uniform policy throughout the country. The centralization of poor law administration through a Poor Law Board and local elected board was an administrative innovation of the greatest importance which left its mark on the whole pattern of British local government, especially in regard to public health and education. It also raised up a class of honest and efficient local officials and so helped to lay the foundation of the civil service state which was growing up as a necessary counterpart of the industry state.

The policy which this admirable machinery was designed to carry out, however, was entirely negative. It relied on the principle of deterrence—'the terror of a well-regulated workhouse', to quote Captain Nicholls, one of the architects of the system. It was based, moreover, upon a misconception which, if we are to accept Dr. Blaug's analysis,[1] was deliberate: the misconception that supplementary additions to wages under the Speenhamland system were the same as the payment of allowances for large families (usually after the fourth child). The former system, he argues, was essentially a wartime measure and was already on the way out; the latter had long been a feature of poor law administration as a necessary concomitant of rising prices and population. The Report of 1834 made no distinction between them: outdoor relief of any kind to the able-bodied was to cease, even relief to the mother of a bastard child. The parish could bring an action against the putative father, but none of the money was to go to the mother. She was to go to the workhouse.

Two relevant factors were ignored: first that low wages were not, in general, the result of poor law allowances, as was so widely believed, but originally the cause of them; second, that the trade

[1] See M. Blaug, 'The Myth of the Old Poor Law and the Making of the New', *Journal of Economic History*, June 1963, and 'The Poor Law Regent Re-examined', ibid., June 1964.

cycle periodically flooded the labour market already trembling on the verge of saturation and left thousands of wage earners with no alternative to starvation but the poor law. The commercial crises of 1837-42 demonstrated the limitations and the Chartist movement revealed the dangers of the Chadwickian panacea, and in 1852 the workhouse test gave place officially—as it had long done unofficially—to the labour test in times of special difficulty. In normal times the principle of deterrence remained unimpaired and the wage earners and their families continued to live under the dread shadow of the workhouse. However, the shadow was not equally distributed. In 'closed' parishes owned and dominated by a single landlord, it was not greatly to be feared; but in the 'open' parishes to which the superfluous population of the closed parishes were driven as a result of a restriction of building or even the pulling down of cottages in the 'closed' parishes, it was very real. The 'open' parishes provided day labourers—often at the cost of a three-mile walk to work—for the 'closed' parishes and paid double or treble in poor rates. 'To him that hath it shall be given; from him that hath not it shall be taken away.' The English rating system had practised this principle under the Old Poor Law, and the landlords saw to it that nothing was done to weaken it under the New. The latter perpetuated a gross injustice while at the same time taking away the one provision—outdoor relief for the able-bodied —that made it barely tolerable. The responsibility of the New Poor Law for the social stresses of the time can hardly be exaggerated.

In the prosperous years 1835-6 the Poor Law Commissioners succeeded in setting up new poor law boards in the southern counties with their large mixed workhouses instead of the four separate institutions (for men, women, children, and the aged) as originally intended. Poor rates fell, but there is no evidence that wages rose, and the earnings of wives and children, frequently working as gang labourers, were called upon to take the place of the forbidden subsidy from the poor rates. Farmers and landlords were better off, and the saving on poor rates was to some extent ploughed back in the form of agricultural improvement, especially drainage, which raised the demand for labour; but whether there was any increase in the rate of migration is doubtful since the parish— not the union as Chadwick had hoped—remained the unit of settlement and of local taxation until 1865. Complaints of rural over-population continued into the second half of the century, and farmers found it cheaper to share the surplus labour amongst themselves than to force the unwanted labourers into the workhouse. Relief of population pressure came not by the New Poor Law, but by railways and the bounding prosperity of agriculture and industry in the great Victorian boom.

The end of the direct allowance system in the rural parishes had been brought about, but at a high price. In the parishes, both urban and rural, north of the Trent, the problem of able-bodied pauperism was not the allowance system, but cyclical unemployment, and to apply the same system to both areas was an example, in Professor Finer's phrase, of 'a political economist's abstraction'. The tens of thousands of hand-loom weavers still remaining in the villages, the first victims of industrial depressions, regarded the poor law as their rightful source of relief in times of distress; surplus labour moved into the towns in response to demand and if necessary back again under removal orders. In order to reduce the number of removals under the settlement laws parishes frequently arranged to pay for the maintenance of their migrant labourers in the parishes to which they had moved through the medium of agencies appointed for that purpose, and poor law authorities in towns were learning to cope with the problems of periodical unemployment by means of emergency relief schemes.

The attempt of the Poor Law Board to establish the new unions north of the Trent and to apply the workhouse test was regarded as a declaration of war by a godless bureaucracy in the interest of the great manufacturers; it was a Malthusian conspiracy to tear wife from husband, parent from child. The Ten Hour agitation merged into the much larger Anti-Poor Law agitation, and the leadership of the working-class movements of the north passed into the hands of the evangelical Tories, J. R. Stephens, an ejected Methodist minister, Richard Oastler, a Methodist-Anglican, the Revd. G. S. Bull, the Vicar of Bradford, and also John Fielden, the Quaker cotton lord of Todmorden. The ground was well prepared for the ideas and language of the physical force Chartists, and Feargus O'Connor left London to take charge of the northern movement. Here, Chartism was in essence a protest against the vain attempt to drive surplus labour upon a market that was already saturated by cyclical unemployment; the proposals of the New Poor Law were felt to be not only a mockery but an insult to the Christian conscience, and the people of the north would have none of it. The new Board of Guardians in Huddersfield was forcibly dispersed three times in six months under the eyes of the magistrates; Oldham and Rochdale made a violent and successful resistance; Bradford staged a minor revolution, and the granting of outdoor relief, even to the able-bodied, had to go on in return for the performance of a labour test.

In 1844 the number of workhouse inmates in the whole country was 234,000, the great majority in the south of England; those relieved outside the workhouse numbered 1,247,000. In 1850 one million people were on relief, or 7 per cent of the population; in 1860 the number was 860,000 or 4·3 per cent and of these indoor recipients numbered 110,000 and 125,000 respectively. In a circular of 1852 to poor law boards, the central authorities admitted that it was not always expedient to apply the workhouse test, even in the case of the able-bodied, and the partial substitution of the labour test for the workhouse test was given official sanction.

The Lancashire cotton famine saw new experiments in the more imaginative use of unemployed labour and it also revived the Elizabethan provision of grants-in-aid from rich parishes to poor parishes. The experience of the Lancashire public works pro-gramme led to the Act of 1862 which empowered the Public Works Loans Commissioners to lend to Poor Law Union and local autho-rities for drainage and similar projects of public utility to absorb unemployed labour. But the principles of 1834 had taken deep root, and Boards of Guardians could see no difference between a pauper doing task work in return for relief and an unemployed man want-ing help to tide him over a period of unemployment. The fall in the ratio of those in receipt of relief continued, partly as a result of the tightening-up of administration under the influence of triumphant individualism of the boom years; and it was even hoped that the advance of prosperity and the spread of the habits of thrift might do away with pauperism and the necessity of the poor law altogether.

The advance of prosperity was not in dispute and the spread of habits of thrift could be measured in terms of friendly societies and savings banks which were registered under various Acts, apart from the many unregistered institutions of which no official cognizance was taken. The total membership of registered friendly societies appears to have grown from 600,000–700,000 in 1801 to 925,000 in 1812 and 1,500,000 in the late 1840s, or 27 per cent of the male population over 20 years of age. There were large semi-federal groups like the Manchester Unity of Oddfellows with a membership of 260,000 in 1848, and a large number of unenrolled burial clubs, village clubs, collecting societies, with a membership extending from parsons and doctors to farm labourers, but wage earners subject to periodical unemployment were less able to maintain their contributions than those, such as domestic servants, who were in receipt of regular if lower wages. There were also over a million depositors in savings banks in 1844, with £27 m. to their credit, of which perhaps half came from the savings of wage earners. There were a few scattered co-operative societies which kept alive the Owenite dream of a regenerated society, and by 1851 there may have been 130 small societies on the Rochdale model with a total membership of 15,000. A powerful and widespread movement of self-help existed among the wage-earning classes, but both religion and economic orthodoxy decreed that it should stand alone; the function of the State was to guard the funds of the enrolled societies, but it left the unenrolled friendly societies to get along as best they could. It should be noted, also, that the societies themselves put up a strenuous resistance to any form of State interference, and the decision to apply to them the rigid principles of *laissez-faire* was one which the societies themselves emphatically endorsed.

The strength of the individualist tradition in working class self-help met its first serious test in 1874 when a distinguished committee of bishops, peers, and M.P.s recommended the formation of a National Friendly Society for the purpose of buying annuities and insurance against sickness and old age through the Post Office, and in 1878 the Revd. W. L. Blackley inaugurated his campaign for a compulsory system of insurance financed by all workers between the ages of 17 and 21 for the provision of sick pay and old-age pensions. It was condemned as unsound and contrary to the spirit of individualism; it was also opposed by the friendly societies which saw in it a rival to the principle of voluntary thrift in which they now had a vested interest. The upper ranks of the wage-earning classes could now provide for themselves, and they were not interested in extending their provisions of security to those who were unable or unwilling to take what was already offered.

Another form of self-help which followed a somewhat similar course was the system of 'the tramping artisan'. Skilled men enhanced their bargaining power and reduced employment in slack times by organizing, through their trade unions, a network of points of call which enabled them to move from town to town in search of employment or higher wages. They could be sure of lodgings and subsistence and, in fact, of 'nomadic unemployment relief', in periods of bad trade. Temporary migration provided a possible escape from a slump until the advance of technology had reduced all the main sectors of industry to subordination to the same market forces. This change began to be felt in some of the more highly organized branches of industry before the middle of the century, and the idea of 'non-nomadic relief' began to be adopted among the more highly specialized trades. The London Branch of the Boiler Makers introduced out-of-work pay as early as 1836; the efforts made by the unions in Sheffield to keep their members out of the workhouse in the middle years of the century were 'prodigious',[1] but the growth of specialization reduced the alternatives open to the unskilled man and he had to look to a mellowing of workhouse test administration to mitigate the growing terrors of unemployment.

All these forms of self-help by the wage earners were facets of the most important social phenomenon of the age of industrialism, the organized working-class movement under the leadership of the trade unions. The removal of the legal ban upon trade unions in 1824-5 was one of the earliest and most notable of the victories won by the Benthamite radicals; they expected that the enjoyment of freedom would quickly demonstrate the futility of using it to promote actions so contrary to the self-interest of the trade unionists themselves. Was it not evident, in view of the limited funds available for wages after rent and profits had had their share, that any advantage of one group could only be obtained at the expense of another? And if wages were forced upwards by successful trade union action, what could the trade unions do to prevent the flight of capital from industry to more profitable fields or to mere hoarding; and what remedy had they for the rise in population that, in the existing state of public enlightenment, would inevitably follow and swallow up the gain?

[1] See S. Pollard, *A History of Labour in Sheffield* (1960).

The workmen were reluctant pupils of these doctrines. Francis Place, their leader and self-appointed oracle at the time of the repeal, said that they expected 'a great and sudden rise in wages when the Combination Acts were repealed; not one of them had any idea of the connection between wages and population'. They thought also not only of higher wages but of checking the advance of machinery which was breaking up the traditional way of life based on family labour in the domestic workshop. Trade union activity in these years was largely a rearguard action against the social consequences of machine production, and whatever form the protest took—the Ten Hour Movement, Chartism, Co-operation, even the struggle for the franchise—the object was utopian as well as practical, a nostalgic dream of the past as well as an attempt to make the best of the present.

The network of clubs and friendly societies meeting in public houses provided a loose framework for the growth of a vague working-class consciousness, and the writings of Cobbett and Owen, not to mention those of Hetherington of the *Poor Man's Guardian* and Morrison of *The Pioneer*, gave it vigorous and varied forms of expression. The mechanics institute movement originating in Scotland and reaching London in 1823 started the artisans on the search for formal knowledge, particularly of classical economics, much to the disgust of Cobbett but greatly to the delight of the leaders of the classical school who saw in it the way—and the only way—of working-class progress through self-restraint and self-improvement. Hodgskin, also from Scotland, proclaimed the labour theory of value in his *Labour Defended* (1825); William Thompson joined Owen in a plea for a new order through co-operative societies. In 1829 Thomas Attwood formed the Birmingham Political Union to bridge the dangerous gap that was opening between the middle and working classes.

The cyclical downswing of 1829-31 coincided with unsuccessful strikes of cotton spinners and the formation of the union of all operative spinners of the kingdom—the first of its kind—under the leadership of John Doherty. In 1830 he became the secretary of the National Association for the Protection of Labour which included not only textile workers but potters, millwrights, blacksmiths, mechanics, miners—the first big national union—and the years 1830-1 were marked by a wave of strikes in the industrial districts and the tragic agricultural labourers' revolt in the southern counties. That agricultural labourers should resort to mob rule and incendiarism was both shocking and terrifying, and the government acted against them with a severity which was in marked contrast to its leniency towards the Chartists ten years later: eight labourers were hanged and 450 were transported. The two parallel and sometimes converging movements of industrial agitation and political reform were whipped to fever heat in these years, and while the middle classes gained the franchise in 1832, the disillusioned working classes rallied under Robert Owen to the Grand National Consolidated Trades Union of Great Britain. It achieved one notable demonstration of national working-class unity in its protest against the second savage blow at the expense of the agricultural labourers, the sentences of transportation passed on the Tolpuddle Martyrs in 1834 for taking a secret oath of loyalty to their trade union. The demonstration failed of its purpose, and the energy which had been flung into this and many other abortive trade union efforts was captured by the movements for the Ten Hour Bill, for the repeal of the New Poor Law, and for the National Charter.

The organized trade unions which survived the collapse of the Grand Consolidated played an inconspicuous role in the Chartist movement. They may have had 100,000 full contributory members in the early 1840s drawn from the skilled craft unions of masons, millwrights, potters, printers, ironfounders, boilermakers, mechanics, and engineers; and in 1842 the miners of Northumberland and Durham brought the National Miners' Association to life. The pioneer work of William Allan in the formation of the Amalgamated Society of Engineers in 1851 was copied by Robert Applegarth, secretary of the Amalgamated Society of Joiners and Carpenters, and by the organizers of other national federations. By developing the technique of collective bargaining they found that they could often obtain satisfactory local settlements, and by campaigning for parliamentary action they could set in motion processes of change which the most obstinate of employers were powerless to obstruct. By these latter means they were able to obtain the new Master and Servant Act of 1867, the inquiry of 1867-9 into the Sheffield outrages[1] which resulted in a triumphant vindication of the 'new model' unions, and the Trade Union Act of 1871, which gave them

[1] See Pollard, op. cit., pp. 152-8.

full legal status, including the protection of their funds. The Criminal Law Amendment Act forbidding picketing, which followed later that year, brought a mobilization of trade-union strength on a national scale, and London leaders—the Junta— joined with provincial leaders to form the Trades Union Congress and to secure the Act of 1875—the trades unions' charter—granting the right of peaceful picketing and permitting any form of action that was not a punishable offence if committed by an individual, e.g. the collective withdrawal of labour.

Another feature of this more accommodating period of labour relations was the attempt made in various parts of the country to revive the principle of arbitration and to adapt it to the needs of the new industrial economy. In this field, A. J. Mundella won a striking success when, in 1860, he put a stop to a long and bitter dispute in the hosiery industry at Nottingham by establishing an arbitration board of masters and representatives of the men's unions. Other boards quickly followed and met with similar success. They usually provided for an independent chairman or for the calling in of a third party; and conciliation merged into arbitration, as the chairman's casting vote meant the making of an award. In the coalfields of North and South Wales and the iron industries of Middlesbrough, they devised the machinery of the sliding scale which caused wages to vary with the price of the product. Men and masters not only began to negotiate round the same table but to educate one another in their respective problems.

By this time the ease with which communications could be maintained as a result of the railways, penny post, and telegraph had gone far to determining the characteristic structure of English trade unionism on the basis of nation-wide occupational unions, not of localized 'Soviets' in the form of trades councils; and the Trades Union Congress which had actually been founded by the trades councils was destined before the end of the century to become the instrument of the great national unions wielding the 'card vote', and excluding the representatives of the trades councils altogether.

Indirectly the unions had already won their most significant victory in the Franchise Act of 1867. The co-operation of the Junta leaders, particularly Robert Applegarth, with John Bright and the middle-class organizations for political reform, secured the peaceful integration of the working-class movement with the constitutional tradition of British politics and gave it a specifically democratic stamp. From 1867 Britain's democratic choice was taken, and the wisdom with which the unions were led must be given a share of the credit for the high degree of unanimity with which it was made.

The importance of the decision was seen in the last quarter of the century when the problem of falling prices, economic reorganization, foreign competition, and fluctuating employment stimulated the movement of the unskilled under specifically socialist leadership. For the first time in history, the lowest grades of the working population were able to present a claim to a fair share of the national income to which their labour so largely contributed, and to make their voice heard within the political community of the nation to which they had at last been admitted.

What had been the reward of the rank and file of the industrial army in the turbulent advance of the industry state? Whether British living standards were raised before the middle of the century is still in debate. Eminent scholars have spoken of the improvement among the better paid artisans and contrasted them with the masses of unskilled and poorly skilled workers whose incomes were almost wholly absorbed in paying for the bare necessities of life, the prices of which remained high. 'My guess', says Professor Ashton, 'would be that the number of those who were able to share in the benefits of economic progress was larger than the number of those who were shut out from these benefits and that it was steadily growing.' On the other side, it is possible to draw attention to the waves of utter destitution that overwhelmed the poor as a result of periodical unemployment, and to argue that the proportion of those excluded from the benefits was so high that the question of an actual decline of standards for such groups as these cannot be dismissed. In view of the enormous programme of simultaneous investment in industry, transport, and trade, and the limitations of the capital market, together with the political weakness of the working classes in the struggle for a more equal distribution of the national product, it was by no means inevitable that the wage earners should gain at all. But they might have lost a great deal. Colonel Torrens, a leading economist and an Irishman, speaking in 1827 of 'two such contiguous countries' as England and Ireland, said

one of two things must necessarily occur; either the Irish people must be raised to the level of the English or the English degraded to the level of the Irish. The condition of the working classes in England and Scotland cannot be preserved from rapid deterioration unless we divert towards the Colonies the stream of Irish labour which now annually inundates the British market.

Fortunately, the accumulation of capital in England was such as to provide food and shelter for a population in Britain which doubled between 1801 and 1851 and at the same time to find employment for a stream of Irish immigrants and to equip the great majority of them with a fund (according to the latest figure) of £15 per head besides their passage money to the New World. Many thousands of Irish had reason to be profoundly grateful to the British industrial revolution, and the British themselves were twice as numerous, even if the majority were not better off.

Any attempt to put the question of *how well off* to statistical test is made difficult by the absence of a satisfactory cost-of-living index: the Silberling index shows a fall of about 20 per cent between 1820 and 1830 and 25 per cent between 1830 and 1850; but the index consists mainly of raw materials, and omits the item of rent; it includes no potatoes or beer but a large proportion of meat and butter and it takes no account of indirect taxation. A study by Professor Ashton of the cost of a standard diet in Manchester in 1821–31 suggests it may have risen, but the price of tea, coffee, and sugar, and also clothes fell; heavy duties on tea, coffee, and tobacco, and on components for house building, on imported food—bacon, butter, cheese as well as corn—excises on glass, paper, printed goods, leather, calicoes, muslins, all represented the claim made by the State on the poor man's pocket. From the time of Huskisson, the claim was whittled down by piecemeal attacks which lowered the price of numerous articles in the poor man's budget, but there is no evidence of marked increase of consumption *per capita* of tea, tobacco, milk, meat, or white bread. In the 1840s Peel made his frontal attack on the fiscal system by imposing an income tax on the rich which enabled him to lighten the cruel load of indirect taxation on the poor, and working-class living standards moved definitely upwards.

One fact at least is not in dispute, namely that the lowest depths of poverty were touched by those whom the machine had left behind or ignored—the handloom weaver, the framework knitter, the hand-made nailer, the sewing girls, journeymen tailors, finishers in lace and hosiery, working in their own houses or in sweat shops under the tiles or in the attics of fashionable London outfitters. The hosiery workshops as late as 1867 were reported to be working fourteen hours a day and children of five and six were said to be clever at stitching the fingers of gloves 'having been at it for two years'. They were kept up shamefully late on Thursday and Friday; 'Mothers will pin them on their knee to keep them to their work, and if they are sleepy give them a slap on the head to keep them awake.'

The largest non-mechanized group were the farm-workers and, owing to the differential attraction of machine industry between north and south, there were wide margins between the lowest and the highest wage for the same type of work. The two extremes in 1851 were the West Riding with an average of 14s. and south Wiltshire with an average of 7s. Both masters and men in the south complained of an over-supply of labour; rate-payers had evolved a variant of the Speenhamland system by dividing among themselves the surplus labour in proportion to the size of the farms. Only a reduction of numbers could effect a solution of the labourers' problems and Joseph Arch, the organizer of the farm labourers' union in the 1870s, reluctantly turned to the organization of emigration as the most effective answer to the meanness of hard-fisted farmers. Other factors were already working to the same end: in 1865 the poor law union instead of the parish was made the unit of settlement (as it had already become, in fact, in some areas by local arrangement) and the labourer was no longer afraid of losing his settlement by leaving his parish. Above all, the completion of the railway network aided the movement of rural labour to the towns, and between 1850 and 1880 the number of agricultural labourers fell by 20 per cent. From the 1850s the advancing economic tide began to catch up with the agricultural labourers as with most other branches of labour. Between 1850 and 1886, it is calculated that money wages rose by 48 per cent; the rise would have been higher but for the sharp set-back that occurred in some industries after the boom of 1871-3. Coal miners who had pushed up their wages by 60 per cent or more lost most of their gains, but the wages of building workers advanced by 50 per cent, of cotton workers by not less than 48 per cent; of agricultural workers by 40 per cent. There was

F

also a slow but significant fall in the length of the working day; the Factory Act of 1850 which introduced the 60-hour week for women textile workers ordered that work should stop on Saturday at 2 p.m. The example set by the factories made it easier for trade unions to negotiate or fight for a shorter working day, and by the 1870s a 54-hour week with Saturday half day was the rule in most organized trades.

The position of the masses of unorganized casual labour of the towns, however, remained deplorably low. There were 'the poor' and 'the very poor' hanging on the brink of destitution, as Charles Booth found in his *Survey* of 1886; and the progress made in the protection of children by factory acts and education acts enlarged rather than reduced the hard core of poverty. The removal of children under thirteen from the labour market by the Education Acts of 1870 and 1876 and the spread of birth control among the higher social groups left the burden of the large family on the section which could least afford to bear it, and social progress was itself contributing to social differentiation and class division.

The family income of the poor was depleted also by the rise of local rates, but in return should be set the benefits derived from the rising tide of municipal services which must have been reflected in increased earning power: the work of local authorities under health and housing acts, the municipal provision of water, gas, transport, paving, draining, public libraries, parks, museums, and the Poor Law provision of well-built infirmaries and, in some towns, of school meals. Outside the towns, the evil of truck was disappearing; in 1843 Staffordshire miners, in spite of the Act of 1831, were still giving a vivid account of the miseries they and their wives endured from the 'tommy' shops of the small employers; many of them started as butties and, helped by the 'tommy' shop, could edge their way into the industry. 'They want hanging by hundreds', said one blood-thirsty witness. Similar things were being said at the inquiry of 1871. The nailers were still shamefully abused by the trucking 'fogger', often a publican, who paid his workers in bad, dear goods. The company shop had its uses in the remote iron and coal centres, and some witnesses were defending it even in the 1870s, but under the pressure of public opinion and trade union action and the development of the distributing trades, it gradually faded from the industrial landscape.

By the time of Charles Booth's *Survey of London* in 1886, the view began to be held that the prime cause of poverty was not improvidence on the part of the poor but the failure of the economic system to pay the poor a living wage. Distribution, not production, became the watchword; impersonal joint-stock capital, under the control of salaried managers responsible largely to absentee boards of directors, was answered by the workman's claim to a fair share of the product in accordance with need, not the level of profit; the older trade unions were no longer satisfied with wage settlements that rose and fell with the market, and the new unions consciously aimed at supplanting the private owner by the State. It is worthy of note that they rarely thought of taking his place themselves. There are many examples of idealistic individuals and groups attempting to establish workers' control; there is at least one example of an employer, a disciple of Ruskin, voluntarily handing over part of his business to his workmen; but they all failed. The example of the Oldham Limiteds described elsewhere[1] is the exception that proves the rule that ownership and control by workers offered no effective alternative to the system of production that had made Britain the workshop of the world. To quote from the recent study of Professor Phelps Brown:

Enterprise was a factor of production that was indispensable not inimical to labour. It could operate only where, within limits much wider than co-operation allowed, it had executive discretion. . . . Many unionists might resent the power of the employer who was seeking his own profit by using them, but when they thought of replacing him, it was by another boss, 'the state', not by themselves.[2]

The entrepreneur with whom this brief study began, is not less present and necessary at the end, although his function is diffused through the impersonal organism of the limited liability company.

---

[1] See above, p. 25.
[2] E. H. Phelps Brown, *The Growth of British Industrial Relations* (1959), pp. 214, 215.

Bibliography

VALUABLE GUIDES to further reading may be found in a number of well-known monographs, particularly Arthur Redford, *The Economic History of England 1760–1860* (ed. W. H. Chaloner, 1960); W. H. B. Court, *A Concise Economic History of Modern Britain* (1953); and Phyllis Deane, *The First Industrial Revolution* (1965).

The reader who wishes to place the economic history of the period in its wider political and social context cannot do better than consult the volumes of Elie Halévy, *The History of the English People*, Vols. I–IV; Asa Briggs, *The Age of Improvement* (1959); and perhaps especially S. G. Checkland, *The Rise of Industrial Society in England* (1964); a study of the contemporary European and American development is given in *The Cambridge Economic History of Europe*, Vol. VI, Parts I and II. The essential foundation for the economic history of the period is provided by the works of Sir John Clapham, especially *The Economic History of Modern Britain*, Vol. I, *The Railway Age* (1926), Vol. II, *Free Trade and Steel* (1932); A. D. Gayer, W. W. Rostow, and A. J. Schwartz, *The Growth and Fluctuation of the British Economy*, 2 vols. (1953); and Phyllis Deane and W. A. Cole, *British Economic Growth 1700–1850* (2nd edition 1967). For stimulating discussions of the process of industrialization see Phyllis Deane and H. J. Habakkuk in *The Economics of Take-off into Sustained Growth* (1965), ed. W. W. Rostow, and H. J. Habakkuk, *American and British Technology in the 19th Century* (1962). These can be supplemented by contemporary sources: G. R. Porter, *The Progress of the Nation* (1851), and J. R. McCulloch, *A Descriptive and Statistical Account of the British Empire*, 2 vols. (1854 edn.); and by the collection of documents edited by G. M. Young and W. D. Hancock, *English Historical Documents 1833–1874*, Vol. XIII (1) (1956). Among the most vivid contemporary accounts are Friedrich Engels, *The Condition of the*

Working Class in England (1844), (translated and edited by W. O. Henderson and W. H. Chaloner, 1958), and Karl Marx, *Capital* (Everyman Edition, 1934). Alongside these, other contemporary accounts should also be read, e.g. Andrew Ure, *Philosophy of Manufactures* (1835); R. H. Greg, *The Factory Question and the Ten Hours Movement* (1837); W. Cooke Taylor, *Tour through the Manufacturing Districts of Lancashire* (1842). For an important comment on the historiography of the period, see T. S. Ashton, 'The Treatment of Capitalism by the Historians' in *Capitalism and the Historians* (ed. F. A. Hayek, 1954). Underlying economic trends are discussed by W. W. Rostow, *British Economy of the Nineteenth Century* (1948) and *Stages of Economic Growth* (1959), and, in a wider context, by W. Ashworth, *A Short History of the International Economy 1850–1950* (1952). Three valuable recent articles of a general nature are: S. Pollard, 'Investment, Consumption and the Industrial Revolution' (*The Economic History Review*, December 1958); Charles Wilson, 'The Entrepreneur in the Industrial Revolution in Britain' (*History*, June 1957); and E. A. Wrigley, 'The Supply of Raw Materials in the Industrial Revolution' (*Econ. Hist. Rev.*, August 1962); and for the last phase of the period, see H. L. Beales, 'The Great Depression in Industry and Trade' (*Econ. Hist. Rev.*, 1934); A. E. Musson, 'The Great Depression in Britain 1873–1896: A re-appraisal' (*The Journal of Economic History*, XIX, June 1959); and especially Charles Wilson, 'Economy and Society in Late Victorian Britain' (*Econ. Hist. Rev.*, August 1965). For some of the historical statistics of the period see W. Hoffmann, *British Industry 1700–1950* (1955), together with the critical article by W. A. Cole, 'The Measurement of Economic Growth' (*Econ. Hist. Rev.*, December 1958); Phyllis Deane, 'Contemporary Estimates of the National Income' (First Half; Second Half of the Nineteenth Century) (*Econ. Hist. Rev.*, April 1956 and April 1957); and B. R. Mitchell and Phyllis Deane, *Abstract of British Historical Statistics* (1962). See also A. L. Bowley, *Wages in England in the Nineteenth Century* (1900); N. J. Silberling, 'British Prices and Business Cycles' (*Review of Economic Statistics*, Vol. V, Supplement 2, 1923); W. T. Layton and G. Crowther, *An Introduction to the Study of Prices* (1938); and the massive but invaluable *History of Prices* by Thomas Tooke and Wm. Newmarch with Introduction by T. E. Gregory, six vols. in four (1928).

Recent local and business studies have added much to our knowledge of the period, and among them the following may be found especially useful: A. H. John, *The Industrial Development of South Wales 1750–1850* (1950); T. C. Barker and J. R. Harris, *A Merseyside Town in the Industrial Revolution, St. Helens 1750–1900* (1954); J. D. Marshall,

Furness and the Industrial Revolution (1958); J. H. Morris and L. J. Williams, *The South Wales Coal Industry* (1958); S. Pollard, *A History of Labour in Sheffield* (1959); S. D. Chapman, *The Early Factory Masters* (1967). Three valuable business histories are: R. S. Fitton and A. P. Wadsworth, *The Strutts and the Arkwrights 1758–1830* (1958); E. M. Sigsworth, *The Black Dyke Mills* (1958); and Charles Wilson, *The History of Unilever*, 2 vols. (1954).

The study of particular industries has been the subject of a valuable bibliography by H. L. Beales, 'The Basic Industries of Britain: Studies in Bibliography IV' (*Econ. Hist. Rev.*, April 1935). Some important later works are: D. L. Burn, *The Economic History of Steel Making 1867–1939* (1940); Charlotte Erickson, *British Industrialists; Steel and Hosiery 1850–1950* (1958); D. C. Coleman, *The Paper Industry 1495–1860* (1958); W. E. Minchinton, *The Tin Plate Industry* (1957); and Alan Birch, *The History of the British Iron and Steel Industry 1784–1879* (1967). An unpublished thesis that can be consulted with profit is D. A. Furnie, *A History of the English Cotton Industry 1784–1879* (Manchester, 1954). For the study of a famous iron-master see J. D. Evans, 'The Uncrowned Iron King' (*National Library of Wales*, (7) 1951–2) and *The Crawshay Dynasty* by John P. Addis (1957). W. O. Henderson, *Britain and Industrial Europe 1750–1870* (1954), traces the impact of British industrial development on Europe. For engineering it is still necessary to go to S. Smiles, *Lives of the Engineers*, 3 vols. (1871–9), but see also: Charles Wilson and William Reader, *Men and Machines, A History of D. Napier and Sons, Engineers, 1808–1958* (1958) and A. E. Musson, 'James Nasmyth and the Early Growth of Mechanical Engineering' (*Econ. Hist. Rev.*, August 1959). Three excellent studies by L. T. C. Rolt, *Thomas Telford* (1958), *Isambard Brunel* (1958), *George and Robert Stephenson: The Railway Revolution* (1960) should be consulted. Books on railways are listed in the monographs mentioned in paragraph 1 above, but see especially: W. T. Jackman, *The Development of Transportation in England* (2 vols.) with Introduction by W. H. Chaloner (1962). On the financing of railways see two recent articles: H. Pollins, 'The Marketing of Railway Shares in the First Half of the Nineteenth Century' (*Econ. Hist. Rev.*, December 1954), and S. A. Broadbridge, 'The Early Capital Market and the Lancashire and Yorkshire Railway' (*Econ. Hist. Rev.*, December 1955).

Among the basic books on agriculture and agricultural policy are Lord Ernle, *English Farming Past and Present* (1936 edn.); J. D. Chambers and G. E. Mingay, *The Agrarian Revolution 1750–1850* (1966); W. Hasbach, *A History of the English Agricultural Labourer* (1920); D. G. Barnes, *History of the English Corn Laws* (1930); C. R. Fay, *The Corn Laws and*

Social England (1934); and perhaps especially J. Caird, *English Agriculture 1850–1* (1852). Among recent contributions are J. A. Scott Watson and M. E. Hobbs, *Great Farmers* (1951); Robert Trow-Smith, *British Livestock Husbandry 1700–1900* (1959) and *English Husbandry* (1951) (containing useful reading list); and articles by G. E. Fussell and M. Compton, 'Agricultural Adjustments after the Napoleonic Wars' (*Econ. History*, 1939); G. E. Fussell, 'Science and Agriculture' in C. J. Singer (ed.), *History of Technology*, Vol. IV (1958); J. D. Chambers, 'Enclosures and Labour Supply in the Industrial Revolution' (*Econ. Hist. Rev.*, 1953); C. S. Orwin and B. J. Fulton, 'A Century of Wages and Earnings' in *The Journal of the Royal Agricultural Society* (92), 1931; and T. W. Fletcher 'The Great Depression of English Agriculture 1872–1896' (*Econ. Hist. Rev.*, 1961). On nineteenth-century landlords see David Spring, 'The English Landed Estate in the Age of Coal and Iron 1830–1880' (*The Journal of Economic History*, 1951, No. 1), and F. M. L. Thomson, *The English Landed Interest in the 19th Century*, 1963.

For a good short account of finance and trade, with some useful figures and excellent reading-list, see J. F. Rees, *A Short Fiscal and Financial History of England* (1921). Recent studies of foreign trade are: A. Redford, *Manchester Merchants and Foreign Trade 1794–1939*, 2 vols. (1934; 1956); A. H. Imlah, *Economic Elements in the Pax Britannica* (1958); S. B. Saul, *Studies in British Overseas Trade* (1960). See also C. E. Fayle, *A Short History of the World's Shipping Industry* (1934); N. S. Buck, *Anglo-American Trade* (1934); W. O. Henderson, *The Lancashire Cotton Famine 1861–1865* (1934); A. L. Dunham, *The Anglo French Treaty of Commerce of 1860* (1930); and articles by H. J. Habakkuk, 'Free Trade and Commercial Enterprise' in *The Cambridge History of the British Empire*, Vol. II (1940), and S. Pollard, 'Laissez Faire and Shipbuilding' (*Econ. Hist. Rev.* (i), 1952). On commercial fluctuations see W. W. Rostow mentioned above, R. C. O. Matthews, *A Study in the Trade Cycle 1833–1842* (1954) and 'The Trade Cycle 1790–1850' in *Oxford Economic Papers*, vol. 6, February 1954; N. Ward-Perkins, 'The Commercial Crisis of 1847' (*Oxford Economic Papers*, 1947) and J. R. T. Hughes, *Fluctuations in Trade, Industry and Finance 1850–1860* (1960). Questions of policy are treated in Lucy Brown, *The Board of Trade and the Free Trade Movement 1830–1842* (1958) and N. McCord, *The Anti-Corn Law League 1838–1846* (1958).

On banking problems, Walter Bagehot's *Lombard Street, A Description of the Money Market* should still be read. Among the more valuable recent works are: Sir John Clapham, *The Bank of England*, Vol. II (1944); E. V. Morgan, *The Theory and Practice of Central Banking* (1942); W. T. C. King, *The London Discount Market* (1936); R. S. Sayers and

T. S. Ashton, *Papers on Monetary History* (1953); D. H. McGregor, *Public Aspects of Finance* (1939); A. K. Cairncross, *Home and Foreign Investments* (1953); L. S. Pressnell, *Country Banking in the Industrial Revolution* (1956). The growth of limited liability is dealt with in G. H. Evans, *British Corporation Finance 1775-1850: A Study of Preference Shares* (1936), and B. C. Hunt, *The Development of the Business Corporation in England* (1936), and in a number of articles, especially H. A. Shannon, 'The Coming of General Limited Liability' and 'The Limited Companies of 1866-1883', both in *Essays in Economic History*, ed. E. Carus Wilson (1954), and John Saville, 'Sleeping Partnerships and Limited Liability 1850-1856' (*Econ. Hist. Rev.*, April 1956). L. H. Jenks, *The Migration of British Capital* (1927), is still indispensable for the early history of foreign investments.

On labour mobility and the growth of towns see A. Redford, *Labour Migration in England* (1926); J. L. and Barbara Hammond, *The Age of the Chartists* (1930); John Saville, *Rural Depopulation* (1954); William Ashworth, *Genesis of British Town Planning* (1954); and E. W. Cooney, 'The Origins of the Victorian Master Builders' (*Econ. Hist. Rev.*, December 1955). The best introduction to the study of population movements is still G. T. Griffith, *Population Problems in the Age of Malthus* (2nd edn. 1967 with Introduction); but for the underlying problems and sources students should consult D. V. Glass, 'Population Movements in England and Wales 1700-1850' in *Population and History*, ed. D. V. Glass and D. E. C. Eversley (1965); W. A. Armstrong, 'La Population de l'Angleterre et du Pays de Galles (1789-1815)', *Annales de Démographie Historique* (1965) (*Études et Chroniques*); and also T. McKeown and R. G. Brown, 'Medical Evidence relating to English Population Changes in the Eighteenth Century' (*Population Studies*, Vol. IX, Nov. 1955), J. T. Krause, 'Changes in English Fertility and Mortality 1781-1850' (*Econ. Hist. Rev.*, August 1958, XI (1)), H. J. Habakkuk, 'The Economic History of Modern Britain' (*The Journal of Economic History*, December 1958), and P. E. Razzell, 'Population Change in Eighteenth Century England: A Re-interpretation' (*Econ. Hist. Rev.*, August 1965); and for a valuable study of contemporary ideas on population see D. E. C. Eversley, *Social Theories of Fertility and the Malthusian Debate* (1959). See also D. C. Marsh, *The Changing Social Structure of England and Wales 1871-1951* (1958).

The current discussion of changes in living standards is represented by T. S. Ashton, 'The Standard of Life of Workers in England 1790-1830' in *Capitalism and the Historians*, ed. Hayek (1954), and E. J. Hobsbawm, 'The British Standard of Living 1790-1850' (*Econ. Hist. Rev.*, August 1956) and is summarized in two well documented studies:

A. J. Taylor, 'Progress and Poverty in Britain' (*History*, February 1960), and R. M. Hartwell, 'Interpretations of the Industrial Revolution' (*The Journal of Economic History*, XIX (2), June 1959). On working-class history the writings of S. and B. Webb, J. L. and Barbara Hammond, and G. D. H. Cole and Max Beer are too well known to need citation. For more recent works see E. H. Phelps Brown, *The Growth of British Industrial Relations* (1959); A. Aspinall, *The Early English Trade Unions* (1949); J. Saville (ed.), *Democracy and the Labour Movement* (1954); Asa Briggs (ed.), *Chartist Studies* (1959) and *Victorian People* (1954); E. Hobsbawm, *Labouring Men: Studies in the History of Labour* (1964); E. P. Thomson, *The Making of the English Working Class* (1963); and 'Time, Work-Discipline, and Industrial Capitalism', *Past and Present* 38, Dec. 1967. See also S. Pollard, *The Genesis of Modern Management: a study of the Industrial Revolution in Great Britain* (1965), Frances Collier, *The Family Economy of the Working Classes in the Cotton Industry* (ed. R. S. Fitton, 1965), and N. J. Smelser, *Social Change in the Industrial Revolution: the application of theory to the Lancashire Cotton Industry 1770-1840* (1959). For social policy see S. and B. Webb, *The Old Poor Law* (1927) and *The Last Hundred Years* (2 vols. 1929); S. E. Finer, *Life and Times of Edwin Chadwick* (1952); M. Simey, *Charitable Effort in Liverpool in the Nineteenth Century* (1951); M. W. Thomas, *The Early Factory Legislation* (1948); C. Driver, *Tory Radical, the Life of Richard Oastler* (1946); R. H. Webb, 'A Whig Inspector: H. S. Tremenheere' (*Journal of Modern History* (27), (1953); Henry Parris, 'The Nineteenth Century Revolution in Government—a Reappraisal Reappraised' (*The Historical Journal*, III (1) 1960); and for a useful introduction to the powerful religious element in social attitudes see R. F. Wearmouth, *Methodism and Working Class Movements of England 1800-50* (1947), and D. Roberts, *Victorian Origins of the British Welfare State* (1960). Vivid contemporary pictures will be found in Peter Quennell (ed.), *Mayhew's London* (no date), E. Hyams (ed.), *Taine's Notes on England* (1957). See also T. Humphry Ward, *The Reign of Queen Victoria*, 2 vols. (1887); *Fortunes Made in Business* (by various authors), 3 vols. (1884); and *Early Victorian England 1830-1865*, 2 vols. (1934), ed. G. M. Young, containing the famous 'Portrait of an Age'.

Index

Africa, 26, 67, 78
agriculture, 9–11, 48–59; labour in, 139–41, 146–7, 151
Allan, William, 147
allotment schemes, 131
allowances, 52, 140
America, U.S.A., 11, 41, 60, 61, 63–4, 65, 67–8, 76, 77–8, 80–1, 106, 111–13
America, North, 63, 67
America, South, 42, 63, 65, 67
Anti-Corn Law League, 50, 71, 108
Applegarth, Robert, 147, 148
arbitration boards, 148
Arch, Joseph, 151
Argentine, the, 41
Arkwright, Sir Richard, 3, 6, 21
Armstrong, William, 43
Ashton, T. S., 3, 149
Asia, 26, 63, 67
Attwood, Thomas, 7, 86, 104, 146
Australia, 77, 78, 81–2

Bacon, Anthony, 31
Bagehot, W., 84
Baines, Edward, 14, 64, 84, 134
balance of payment, 68, 75, 79
bank Acts, 86, 88, 90, 91, 108
Bank of England, 86, 88–90, 94–5, 104–5, 109–10, 111
bank rate, 91–2, 114
Banking School, 88, 90
Bentham, Jeremy, 132–3, 136–8
Bessemer, 10, 34
bicycle, 43

bills of exchange, 83, 85, 93, 104, 106
Birkinshaw, J., 36
Birmingham, 7, 12, 19, 43
birth-rate, 116–18
black band ironstone, 32
'Black Friday', 112
'blind', capital, 94, 96, 112. See also capital
Board of Guardians, 143
Board of Trade, 6, 38, 39, 65, 66, 68, 70, 73, 97
Bolckow, Vaughan, 33, 34
boot and shoe factories, 43
Booth, Charles, 152, 153
Bowring, Dr. John, 6, 66
Brassey, Thomas, 41, 108
Brazil, 108
Briggs, Professor Asa, 7
Bright, John, 138, 148
Brunel, I. K., 20
Bubble Act, 93, 95
Bull, G. S., 8, 143
butties, 13

Caird, James, 37, 55
Cairncross, Professor, 44, 75
Canada, 78
canals, 36, 40
capital: investment of, 4–5, 9–10, 30, 38, 44, 92–9, 103–4; export of, 60, 68, 75, 78, 106–7, 110, 130–1
cash payments, 65
Chadwick, Edwin, 124, 133n., 138, 141
Chamberlain, Joseph, 55, 127

Chartists, 69, 71, 108, 109, 143
cheques, 89, 104
Child Labour, 6; acts regarding, 137-9
China, 26, 67, 111
Christian Socialists, 97-8
City of Glasgow Bank, 92, 98
Clannie, W. R., 29
Clapham, Sir John, 17, 18, 24, 47, 63, 77, 85
classical economics, 55, 134, 135, 146
Clearing House, 39
Cleveland, 33
coal industry, 28-31, 113; and export, 30-1, 62, 76, 81; and railways, 37, 41; and miners, 139, 147, 151
Cobbett, William, 47, 86, 104, 146
Cobden, Richard, 71, 76, 80
Cockerill Bros., 3
coffee, 63, 85
collective bargaining, 147
collectivism, 136, 138
Colling, Charles, 47
Combination Acts, 145, 146
commission agent, 85
consumption industries, 99-100
co-operation, 25, 97-8, 144
Corn Law of 1815, 54, 62, 64, 70
cotton industry and trade, 11, 12, 13, 14-27, 62, 75-6, 77, 84, 104-5, 106, 109, 112
country banks, 53, 83, 87, 111.
Crawshaw, Richard, 7
—— William, 7, 31, 94
Crimean War, 74, 75, 77, 91, 110-11
crises: in England, 85-8, 89-90, 91-3, Ch. VI; in U.S.A., 107, 111
Cromford, 21
Crystal Palace, 71
currency and Currency School, 87, 89, 90, 91
customs, 63, 69
cutlery trades, 13, 43
Cyfarthfa, 7, 31

Davy, Humphry, 29
death-rate, 116-18; London, 127-8
Devonshire, Duke of, 7, 10
discount market, 85, 88, 91
dissenters, academies, 8; chapels, 133
doctors, 116
domestic servants, 15
Dowlais, 7, 31

East India Company, 63, 67, 89, 109
education, 136, 139; Acts, 138; technical, 6, 80
Egypt, 78
electricity, 44, 80
Ellman, John, 47
emigration and migration, 128-9
Empire countries, 26, 67, 76, 78, 81
Engels, F., 138
engineers, 19-21, 43, 44
entail, 56
entrepreneur, 5-8, 153
'equities', 95
Europe, 61, 63, 65, 66, 67, 76, 78
excise, 62, 64, 69
exports, 11, 12, 30, 61-3, 106

factory production, 14, 123-4, 136-7
factory Acts, 134-5, 136, 137
Fairbairn, William, 19, 20, 42
'Fair Traders', 80
family firm, 100
Faraday, Michael, 7, 29, 44
fens, 47
fiduciary issue, 90, 92
Fielden, J., 142
Finer, Professor, 142
four-course rotation, 46, 48, 53
free trade, 16, 57, 64, 75-6, 109
friendly societies, 132, 143-4
'futures', 77

Galloway, Robert, 29
Game Laws, 52
Germany and German competition, 27, 60, 66, 76, 80
Giffen, Sir Robert, 80
Gilchrist, Thomas, 34
Gladstone, W. E., 73-4, 97
Glass, Professor, 117n.
gold discoveries, 109-10
Goschen, Mr., 74
Gott, Benjamin, 6
Great Depression, 26, 44, 82, 100, 103
Greg, R. H., 6, 136
Guest, Sir Josiah, 7

harvest, influence of, 54, 55, 102, 107, 109
health and housing, 122, 124-6, 127; Acts of, 126, 139; Board of, 124, 138
Hill, Octavia, 125, 127
Holland, 77
Horner, Leonard, 23, 137
hosiery, 27, 28; workers, 14
Huddersfield, 143
Hume, Deacon, 70
Hume, Joseph, 64
Hungry Forties, 72, 108
Huskisson, William, 65

Imlah, A. H., 67
imports, 63, 67, 73, 76, 79, 85
Improvement Commissioners, 116, 123
income tax, 58, 62, 68-71, 73
India, 42, 78-9, 81, 110
individualism, 132
Inman, William, 42
inspectorate, 135-6, 138-9
'invisible earnings', 61, 67-8, 78-9, 81
Ireland and the Irish, 23, 25, 72, 128, 134, 149
iron clads, 111
iron industry and trade, 31-5, 76, 79, 81, 94, 99, 100, 111, 121

Jevons, Stanley, 30
joint-stock banks, 86-7, 94, 98
joint-stock companies, 104
Junta, 148

Kay-Shuttleworth, Dr. (Kay), 106, 119, 120, 138, 139
Krause, J. T., 118
Krupp, Alfred, 31

labour, Ch. VIII; casual, 123, 152; conditions, 6, 105, 107-9, 115, 130; migration, 119-20, 130; self-help, 143-4; standard of life, 149-53
Laissez-faire, 78, 95, 138, 144
land-lords, 9-11, 55, 56-7, 62
Lawes, John, 48, 57
ley farming, 48
Lister, Samuel Cunliffe, 24
Liverpool, Lord, 65
Lloyd's marine insurance, 93

Malthus, Thomas, 117, 131, 132, 133
Manchester merchants, 89
marriage, age of, 118
Marx, Karl, 4
Matthews, R. C. O., 63
Maudslay, Henry, 19, 20, 42
Mechanics Institute Movement, 146
mechanization—wool, worsted, 23; coal, 28; hosiery, 27; shoes, 43
Merthyr Tydfil, 7
Middlesbrough, 7, 33, 34
Morley, I. and R., 14, 27
Mundella, A. J., 148; and Hine, 27
Municipal Corporations Act, 125
Murdoch, William, 19
Mushet, David, 32

Napier, David, 19, 42
Nasmyth, James, 19, 20
National Debt, 74, 86, 87
Navigation Acts, 41, 65, 68, 73
Neilson, James, 32
Newcastle on Tyne, 122
New Lanark, 21
New Zealand, 78
Norwich, 15, 37
Nottingham, 132, 148

Oastler, Richard, 134, 142
O'Connor, Feargus, 142
old age pensions, 144
Oldham Ltds., 25-6, 98-9, 153
Orient, 64
overcrowding, 126. See Health
overdrafts, 89
Overend, Gurney & Co., 85, 112
Owen, Robert, 6, 21, 123, 146

Palmer, Horsley, 88, 89, 90
Parliamentary Train, 39
Parnell, Henry, 68, 70
Peel, Sir Robert, 6, 55, 70, 71, 72, 73, 108
Perkins, William, 43
Peto, Morton, 41
Phelps-Brown, Professor, 153
Place, Francis, 146
Poor Law, 69, 70, 120, 132, 140, 141, 142-3; Act of 1834, 52, 132, 139-41
population, 15, 52; rise of, 4, 116-19
Porter, G. R., 58, 59, 68
prices, 51, 75-6, 86-7, 109-11, 150-1

Quakers, 8

Railway and Canal Commission, 39
railway iron, 31, 32-3, 35, 41
railway system, 10, 35-41, 75, 94; and
    speculation, 38, 91, 108-9
railway termini, 126
Rainhill, 36, 106
Ransome of Norwich, 46
reaping machine, 49
refrigeration, 44
Rennie, John and George, 19, 42
rents, 53
Ricardo, 4-5, 62, 86
Rochdale, 98
Rothamsted, 48, 57
Rothschild, 93, 104
Royal Agricultural Society, 56
Royal Dockyards, 42
Royal Show, 57
Russia, 63

Salt, Titus, 124
savings banks, 144
Scandinavia, 63
Scotland, 49, 86, 95, 146
Scragg, John, 49
'scrip', 38, 108
Settlement Laws, 49, 142, 151
sewing machine, 43
Shaftesbury, Lord, 127, 137, 138
Sheffield, 31, 147
Shillibeer, George, 41
shipping, 17n., 41-2, 67, 77, 111
silk, industry and trade, 14, 65
Siemens, William, 34-5, 44
Silberling index, 150
Simon, John, 125, 139
Singapore, 77
Slater, Samuel, 3
slave emancipation, 89
Sliding scale, 54, 70
Small, James, 46
Smith, Adam, 4, 131
smuggling, 66
South Wales, 29
Southwood Smith, 124
Spain, 60
steel, 34-5, 79
Stephens, J. R., 142

Stephenson, George, 29, 36
—— Robert, 36, 106
Stock Exchange, 77, 93
Strutt, Jedediah, 6, 21, 23
Styal, 21
sugar, 85
Sunday schools, 8
Swing, Captain, 49

taxation, 62-4, 69, 73-4
telegraph, 44
telephone, 44
Telford, Thomas, 19
Ten Hour agitation, 142; Bill, 147; Day,
    70; terms of trade, 66, 74, 101-2
threshing machine, 49
Times, The, 33, 38, 96, 138
tin plate, 44
tithes, 51, 53
Todmorden, 6
Tolpuddle Martyrs, 147
Tooke, Thomas, 64, 88
Torrens, Colonel, 91, 139, 149-50; trade,
    foreign, Ch. IV; and tariffs, 60-1; and
    Empire, 66-8, 110-11. See also Board of
    Trade, Sir Robert Peel, etc.
trade cycle, 102-4, 140-1. See also crises
Trade Unions, 134-5, 145-9
tramp steamers, 30
Tremenheere, H. S., 137
truck, 152
turnips, 9, 48
Tyneside, 28-31

unemployment, 134, 142, 143-5, 149. See
    also labour
Ure, Andrew, 20, 32
usury laws, 105

vaccination, 116
Villiers, Charles, 50

wages and wage-earners, 71, 140-1, 144-5,
    150-1. See also labour
wage fund, 55
Wear and Tyne, 30
weavers, 13, 24
Wellington, Duke of, 11, 55

West Indies, 63, 67
West Riding, 24, 25
West Wales, 52
wheat prices, 47, 51. *See also* harvest
Whitehaven, 10
Whitney, Eli, 11
Whitworth, Joseph, 20, 43
Wiggin, Timothy, 85

Wilson, Charles, 18
woolcombing, 25
wool, farmers, 50, 59
workhouses, mixed, 142
worsted, 24–5, 26

Zollverein, 63, 66